"A delightful combination of child-friendly spiritual lessons and fun facts about dogs—two concepts that go hand-in-paw. Kids already know that their furry companions are faithful friends. And *Paws-itive Inspirations* helps them discover that God is the most faithful friend of all."

—**Peggy Frezon**, contributing editor, *All Creatures* magazine; coauthor, *Mini Horse, Mighty Hope*; author, *The Dog in the Dentist Chair*

"This devotional will have a fur-ever place on my shelf! I can't wait to get a copy for my granddaughter who is a dog fanatic. It's the perfect balance of dog stories and biblical takeaway, with a lot of tail-wagging moments, as well. I also learned a lot about the various breeds while reading. Highly recommended for dog lovers, young and old!"

—**Janice Thompson**, author, *Paws for Reflection: Fifty Devos for Dog Moms*

"I have been privileged throughout my life to work with animals of various shapes and sizes. I have always felt that we as humans can certainly learn many things from our pets when it comes to how God intended us to live and treat each other. Michelle Medlock Adams and Wendy Hinote Lanier have taken the time and effort to write out these lessons in a way that is fun, educational, and inspirational for people of all ages. Kids and adults will enjoy learning new facts about individual breeds as well as how they exemplify God's faithfulness, mercy, and love for everyone who has eyes to see."

—**Jason Beard**, DVM, Hide-A-Way Small Animal Clinic, Lindale, Texas

Michelle Medlock Adams & Wendy Hinote Lanier

Illustrations by William H. Hinote

PAWS-itive
INSPIRATIONS

90 DEVOTIONS
for Kids and Dog Lovers

{revised edition}

Birmingham, Alabama

Paws-itive Inspirations
Previously published as *Puppy Dog Devotions: 75 Fun Fido Facts, Bible Truths, and More!*

Iron Stream Kids
An imprint of Iron Stream Media
100 Missionary Ridge
Birmingham, AL 35242
IronStreamMedia.com

Copyright © 2021, 2024 by Michelle Medlock Adams and Wendy Hinote Lanier

No part of this publication may be reproduced, stored in a retrieval system, or transmitted in any form or by any means—electronic, mechanical, photocopying, recording, or otherwise—without the prior written permission of the publisher. Iron Stream Media serves its authors as they express their views, which may not express the views of the publisher.

Library of Congress Control Number: 2024942134

All Scripture quotations, unless otherwise indicated, are taken from the Holy Bible, New International Version®, NIV®. Copyright ©1973, 1978, 1984, 2011 by Biblica, Inc.™ Used by permission of Zondervan. All rights reserved worldwide. www.zondervan.com. The "NIV" and "New International Version" are trademarks registered in the United States Patent and Trademark Office by Biblica, Inc.™

Scripture quotation marked AMPC is taken from the Amplified® Bible (AMPC), Copyright © 1954, 1958, 1962, 1964, 1965, 1987 by The Lockman Foundation. Used by permission. www.lockman.org.

Scripture quotations marked CEV are taken from the Contemporary English Version Copyright © 1991, 1992, 1995 by American Bible Society. Used by Permission.

Scripture quotations marked ESV are taken from the ESV® Bible (The Holy Bible, English Standard Version®), copyright © 2001 by Crossway, a publishing ministry of Good News Publishers. Used by permission. All rights reserved.

Scripture quotations marked MSG are taken from *The Message*, copyright © 1993, 2002, 2018 by Eugene H. Peterson. Used by permission of NavPress. All rights reserved. Represented by Tyndale House Publishers.

Scripture quotations marked NKJV are taken from the New King James Version®. Copyright © 1982 by Thomas Nelson. Used by permission. All rights reserved.

Scripture quotations marked NLT are taken from the Holy Bible, New Living Translation, copyright ©1996, 2004, 2015 by Tyndale House Foundation. Used by permission of Tyndale House Publishers, Carol Stream, Illinois 60188. All rights reserved.

Scripture quotations marked NLV are taken from the New Life Version, copyright © 1969 and 2003. Used by permission of Barbour Publishing, Inc., Uhrichsville, Ohio 44683. All rights reserved.

Scripture quotations marked TLB are taken from The Living Bible copyright © 1971. Used by permission of Tyndale House Publishers, Carol Stream, Illinois 60188. All rights reserved.

ISBN-13: 978-1-56309-776-8
Ebook ISBN: 978-1-56309-777-5

1 2 3 4 5—28 27 26 25 24

Dedication

From Michelle

For Bob B. Bridge—"BBB"
the best writer I've ever read, an amazing mentor, a great friend,
and the only person I know who might love dogs more than I do.

Also, in memory of my late dog-loving mother Marion Medlock—
who fed every stray in the neighborhood.
I'm sure your heavenly home is filled with many fur babies.

From Wendy

To all the dogs I've loved who've shown me God's love
and acceptance in its purest form.
I truly believe dogs are God's special gift to us.
They will almost always point us to Him if we take the time to look.

And to my dad—the man who is always there when you need him.
I'm proud to call you my Pop.

Contents

Acknowledgments xi
Introduction xiii
  1. Afghan Hound 2
  2. Airedale Terrier 4
  3. Akita 6
  4. Alaskan Malamute 8
  5. American English Coonhound 10
  6. American Eskimo Dog 12
  7. American Foxhound 14
  8. American Pit Bull Terrier 16
  9. Australian Cattle Dog 18
10. Australian Stumpy Tail Cattle Dog 20
11. Basenji 22
12. Basset Hound 24
13. Beagle 26
14. Bearded Collie 28
15. Belgian Malinois 30
16. Bernese Mountain Dog 32
17. Bichon Frise 34
18. Bloodhound 36
19. Border Collie 38
20. Boston Terrier 40
21. Boxer 42

Contents

22. Bull Terrier 44
23. Bulldog 46
24. Bullmastiff 48
25. Cairn Terrier 50
26. Cane Corso 52
27. Catahoula Leopard Dog 54
28. Cavalier King Charles Spaniel 56
29. Chesapeake Bay Retriever 58
30. Chihuahua 60
31. Chinese Crested 62
32. Chinese Shar-Pei 64
33. Chow Chow 66
34. Cocker Spaniel 68
35. Collie 70
36. Czechoslovakian Vlcak 72
37. Dachshund 74
38. Dalmatian 76
39. Doberman Pinscher 78
40. French Bulldog 80
41. German Shepherd 82
42. German Shorthaired Pointer 84
43. Golden Retriever 86
44. Goldendoodle 88
45. Great Dane 90
46. Great Pyrenees 92
47. Greyhound 94
48. Ibizan Hound 96

49. Irish Setter 98

50. Irish Wolfhound 100

51. Japanese Chin 102

52. Keeshond 104

53. Komondor 106

54. Labradoodle 108

55. Labrador Retriever 110

56. Lhasa Apso 112

57. Maltese 114

58. Maremma Sheepdog 116

59. Mixed Breed 118

60. Newfoundland 120

61. Old English Sheepdog 122

62. Papillon 124

63. Parson Russell Terrier 126

64. Pekingese 128

65. Pembroke Welsh Corgi 130

66. Pomeranian 132

67. Poodle 134

68. Pug 136

69. Puggle 138

70. Puli 140

71. Rat Terrier 142

72. Rhodesian Ridgeback 144

73. Rottweiler 146

74. Russian Toy 148

75. Saint Bernard 150

Contents

76. Samoyed 152
77. Schipperke 154
78. Scottish Deerhound 156
79. Scottish Terrier 158
80. Shetland Sheepdog (Shelties) 160
81. Shih Tzu 162
82. Siberian Husky 164
83. Soft Coated Wheaten Terrier 166
84. Standard Schnauzer 168
85. Weimaraner 170
86. Welsh Terrier 172
87. West Highland White Terrier 174
88. Whippet 176
89. Wire Fox Terrier 178
90. Yorkshire Terrier 180
Conclusion 183
Dog Groups as Recognized by the American Kennel Club 185
Glossary of Competition Terms 187
Notes 189
About the Authors 207

Acknowledgments

Much love and many thanks to William H. Hinote for stepping up to help us with the artwork when we needed him.

Introduction

From the time I was a little girl, I always loved dogs. My sister and my brother were much older, so I grew up like an only child. My best friend? My beloved dachshund named Penny. In fact, she was my only friend for quite some time.

We lived in a nice neighborhood in a small town in southern Indiana, but there were no children who lived nearby. Once or twice a year, a little girl named Angela would visit her father who lived next door, and that was nice. I looked forward to her visits, but two visits a year didn't make for much of a friendship. So Penny became my best friend.

We were inseparable. She was a great playmate. Sometimes, I'd tie a bonnet on Penny's head and drape pearls around her neck. Then I'd put on my floppy hat and my mother's high heels, and we'd have tea parties. Of course, I'd pour real water in Penny's cup and give myself imaginary tea. It was always great fun, and Penny was the perfect guest.

Other times, Penny and I would sit in my sandbox, and I would make up stories. I'd tell her all about the princes and princesses who lived in my tree house. And sometimes, I'd make up stories about her. She liked it when I'd mention her name every so often. She'd wag her tail and give me a lick as if to say, "That's good. Go on. Go on."

Penny was a great cheerleader too. When my dad taught me to ride my bike in the alley behind our house, Penny would bark and run in circles, cheering me on to life without training wheels. When I'd fall and scrape my knee, which I often did, Penny would run to my side and lick away the tears. She was always right by my side.

On my first day of kindergarten, Penny rode with me in the front seat of my mom's car. As I walked away from the car and waved goodbye to that wet nose pressed against the inside of the car window, I smiled just knowing that she'd be waiting for me when I got home.

Introduction

As I grew up, our friendship grew too. I told Penny everything. She was a great listener. She didn't have a huge vocabulary, but her eyes and tail wags spoke volumes. I know in my heart that Penny is in heaven, waiting for me, alongside several other dogs I have loved and said goodbye to over the years—Max, Maddie Anne, Miller, Mollie Mae, and Bella.

My love for dogs has been a lifelong love affair. We've always had a dog or two in our home, and we always will. I'm guessing you love dogs too, or you wouldn't be reading this book. Dogs are the most amazing creatures, aren't they? Dogs love us when we are at our best, and even when we are at our worst. And they seem to bring out the best in us. We can learn a lot from our canine companions as you'll see in the pages of this book.

My coauthor Wendy (also a major dog lover) and I hope that you'll discover some interesting facts about the many breeds covered in this book, as well as be encouraged to grow closer to God. We have included a few features to make it easier to use this devotional:

- **Unleash the Truth** is your key Bible verse for the day. You might even want to memorize it.
- **Digging Deeper** is a section with some questions to ask yourself or maybe even answer in your journal.
- **Fido 411** features a fun or interesting fact about that particular breed.
- **Weekly Tail-Waggers** challenge you to think more deeply about what you've just learned and actually put those lessons into action.

Whether you have your own dog to love or you love puppies from afar, we pray that you enjoy this journey of paws-itivity with us. 😊

   Michelle

Afghan Hound

 Hound

 25 to 27 inches; 50 to 60 pounds

 The Afghan Hound is recognized as one of the oldest breeds of purebred dogs. Despite being bred in remote parts of Afghanistan as a hunting dog, the Afghan Hound became a favorite of the royals and the upper class. It was introduced to the Western world in the 1800s.[1]

 The Afghan Hound won Best in Show at the Westminster Kennel Club Dog Show in 1957 and 1983.

 1927

How Do You Handle Correction?

Originally used for hunting large prey in both the deserts and the mountains of Afghanistan, the Afghan's long fur coat was needed for warmth. The fact that its coat is lovely is just an added bonus. The Afghan is fast and can run great distances, which made it a great hunting companion. Also, it was able to hold off dangerous animals such as leopards, protecting its owners at all costs. Today, not too many Afghans are hunting or defending against leopards. Instead, they are most likely lounging on the family couch. But, make no mistake, this breed may not want to share the couch with you. The Afghan acts a little bit like a cat, only wanting affection on its terms.

Honestly, if the dog world had a supermodel, it would be the Afghan Hound. With its flowing, silky coat, distinct narrow features, and dignified (sometimes standoffish) attitude, the Afghan Hound is a beautiful,

Paws-itive Inspirations

sophisticated dog. But this breed has more than beauty going for it. The Afghan hound is also quite intelligent and a great problem solver. But it's a very stubborn breed, which makes it difficult to train. Here's what else—Afghans are very sensitive animals. They do not respond well to harsh correction, so when you train them, you have to be gentle.

Let's face it. Nobody likes correction—especially harsh correction. But, like the Afghan, we have to be corrected in order to become better. And, the way we receive God's correction and training is by reading the Bible and following His commandments. Without discipline, we can't become the people God has created us to be. Proverbs 12:1 says, "To learn, you must love discipline; it is stupid to hate correction" (NLT). That's pretty clear, isn't it? The best part about God's correction? It's always gentle, and it's always in your best interest. You can trust Him.

**Unleash the Truth:** "No discipline is enjoyable while it is happening—it's painful! But afterward there will be a peaceful harvest of right living for those who are trained in this way." (Hebrews 12:11 NLT)

**Digging Deeper:** How do you feel when someone corrects you? Do you respond with a good attitude, knowing that correction will help you grow into a better person?

Fido 411: Did you know that famed artist Pablo Picasso often featured his Afghan "Kabul" in his paintings? It's true![2]

Weekly Tail-Waggers: The next time your parents or your teacher or someone else close to you corrects you, take notice of how you respond. Are you too sensitive to receive correction? Do you react with a good attitude? Ask God to help you grow in this area.

 *Michelle*

Airedale Terrier

 Terrier

 22 to 24 inches; 50 to 70 pounds

 In the mid-1800s dog breeders in the Aire Valley of Yorkshire, England, needed to come up with a terrier that could hunt rats as well as larger animals. So, they bred Old English black and tan terriers with Otterhounds and a few other breeds to get Airedales, which were originally called waterside or Bingley terriers.[1]

 The Airedale Terrier has won Best in Show four times at Westminster: 1912, 1919, 1922, and 1933.

 1888

Faith for Everyone

Airedale Terriers are friendly, intelligent, and athletic dogs. They are also fiercely loyal and lovers of people, especially one such Airedale named Paddy the Wanderer. Paddy showed up all by himself at the waterfront in Wellington, New Zealand, one day in 1928. The dockworkers had no idea where Paddy had come from or why he was suddenly there all the time, but they soon learned of Paddy's story.

The sweet dog's constant companion, Elsie, had died from a serious illness right before her fourth birthday, and Paddy was in need of new friends to help heal his hurting heart. So, he became buddies with seamen, water taxi drivers, harbor workers, and anyone else who wandered the waterfront. A group of Paddy's new friends all chipped in to pay for the dog's annual license, and they let him go on lots of boat rides as well as appointing him

Paws-itive Inspirations

the nightwatchman of the harbor. Everyone loved Paddy. He never met a stranger, and he brought joy to all he visited. When Paddy died in 1939, a fleet of taxis formed a long funeral procession, and Queens Wharf in Wellington placed a memorial plaque in honor of Paddy the Wanderer next to a special drinking fountain—one for humans and two for dogs.[2]

You might say Paddy left his paw prints on the hearts of many. He made an impact just by being friendly. And guess what? So can you. We can learn several things from Paddy's story. First, Paddy didn't withdraw and become a loner when his heart was hurting. Instead, he showed up where he could meet people and make a difference. When we take our eyes off of our own hurts and focus on others, everybody feels better, and everybody wins. Secondly, Paddy consistently showed up to share his love, and people looked forward to his presence. Be like Paddy—show up and share the love. Be the kind of person whom people look forward to seeing, and when you ooze love, you will be.

Unleash the Truth: "By this everyone will know that you are my disciples, if you love one another." (John 13:35)

Digging Deeper: Have you ever been around someone who just made you feel happy? Why not try to be that person for others? Ask God to help you share His love to everyone you meet.

Fido 411: The Airedale Terrier is one of the largest terrier breeds, and it has been nicknamed "king of the terriers."

Weekly Tail-Waggers: Pray this: "Father God, help me be the kind of person that people are happy to see. Help me share Your love everywhere I go. I love You. Amen."

 *Michelle*

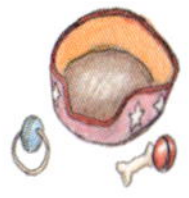

5

Akita

(uh-KEE-tuh)

 Working

 24 to 28 inches; 70 to 130 pounds (Note: Japanese and American Akitas differ in size and weight. The American Akita is slightly larger.)[1]

 Akitas are named for the Akita Prefecture (district or region) of Japan where they originated. They were bred to hunt large game such as boar, deer, and bear.[2]

 Although they have never taken Best in Show at Westminster, Akitas have placed first in the Working group three times. They also excel in obedience, rally, and agility competitions.[3]

  1972

Faithful to the End

Akitas are large, powerful dogs, well-known for their courage and loyalty. They love their families fiercely but strangers—not so much.

In the 1920s, an Akita in Japan became famous all over the world for his devotion and loyalty. Hachiko was the beloved pet of a Japanese professor. Each day Hachiko walked his owner to the train station in Tokyo and waited there all day for him to return. Then one day, a terrible thing happened. The professor died while he was at work.

That day Hachiko waited at the station just as he had every other day, but his owner never came. Every day for more than ten years he waited. During those years, Hachiko became a symbol of love and faithfulness to the people of Japan. When he finally died, the whole country mourned his death. They built a statue to honor him outside the Tokyo train station where he had waited so long.[4]

That kind of loyalty is amazing. Hachiko was faithful to his owner to his dying day. It's a kind of faithfulness that is hard to find in people *or* dogs. But it is exactly the kind of faithfulness we can expect from our heavenly Father. He is *always* faithful, even when we're not.

It's a sad fact: people can sometimes hurt us or let us down. That's just part of being human. Everybody makes mistakes. The great thing is that God never makes a mistake. He never hurts us, and He never lets us down. He always keeps His promises. We can trust Him. He loves us with an everlasting love. And He is always there for us. His faithfulness never ends.

 **Unleash the Truth:** "Your love, Lord, reaches to the heavens, your faithfulness to the skies." (Psalm 36:5)

 **Digging Deeper:** Have you ever felt like someone let you down?

 Fido 411: In 1937 Helen Keller learned the story of the famous Hachiko. She was so impressed she brought the first Akita to the United States.[5]

 Weekly Tail-Waggers: Take time this week to look up the following scriptures: Psalm 57:10; Psalm 86:15; Psalm 91:4; Psalm 100:5; Psalm 119:30; Isaiah 25:1; and Lamentations 3:23. Read them and think about what they mean. God is faithful!

 Wendy

Alaskan Malamute

(MA-luh-myoot)

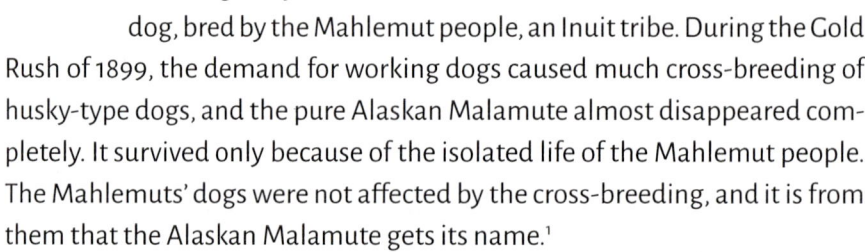

 Working

 23 to 25 inches; 75 to 85 pounds

 The Alaskan Malamute was originally an Artic dog, bred by the Mahlemut people, an Inuit tribe. During the Gold Rush of 1899, the demand for working dogs caused much cross-breeding of husky-type dogs, and the pure Alaskan Malamute almost disappeared completely. It survived only because of the isolated life of the Mahlemut people. The Mahlemuts' dogs were not affected by the cross-breeding, and it is from them that the Alaskan Malamute gets its name.[1]

 The Malamute took the top spot in the Working group in 1998 and has placed in that group ten other times at Westminster.[2] Although the Malamute has never taken a Best in Show, today's Malamutes win titles in working dog programs composed of events such as sledding/carting, packing, and weight pulling.[3]

 1935

Even When We Don't Understand It—God's Way Is Best

Alaskan Malamutes have amazing strength and stamina. They can carry heavy loads over rough terrain in the worst weather conditions imaginable. They are friendly (toward people—other dogs not so much unless well-socialized) and super smart. But in spite of all these great qualities, Malamutes are known as a challenging breed. They can be tough to handle because they often choose to disobey commands if they don't see the point. They want to know the *why* before they are willing to obey.[4]

That's a problem a lot of people have too. When the children of Israel were

Paws-itive Inspirations

wandering in the desert, God gave them a long list of rules to follow. Some of them were about washing their hands and cooking their food. Others were about throwing away cracked pottery. They must have seemed weird at the time. Those kinds of things weren't rules in other cultures. Why was God telling them to do these things? As we know today, God was protecting them from germs. The children of Israel were healthy and disease-free when other cultural groups were not. If the children of Israel had demanded to know why before they obeyed, they might have been sickly too.

The fact is, God can see what we can't. He knows exactly what the future holds. And He would never ask us to do something that would harm us. Maybe God is telling you to be a friend to that new kid at school. Maybe He's telling you to help an elderly neighbor without expecting anything in return. Or maybe He's telling you to help out around the house more. Sometimes the things God wants us to do are not comfortable or what we *want* to do, but they are always what's best for us in the long run. Obedience to God will always work in our favor. We don't always need to know why. But we can be sure that God's plan is *always* to give us hope and a bright future. Our job is to obey Him in all we do—even if we don't see the *why* in it.

Unleash the Truth: "Obedience is better than sacrifice, and submission is better than offering the fat of rams." (1 Samuel 15:22 NLT)

Digging Deeper: How do we know what God wants us to do? (Hint: It's in the book.)

Fido 411: The Alaskan Malamute was adopted as the state dog of Alaska in 2010.[5]

Weekly Tail-Waggers: God speaks to us in many ways. One is through His Word. The book of Proverbs is a good place to find out how we should live our lives. Try reading a chapter of Proverbs each day for a month.

 Wendy

American English Coonhound

 Hound

 23 to 26 inches; 45 to 65 pounds

 Adapted from English Foxhounds brought to the colonies in the 1600s and 1700s, the Coonhound was bred to withstand harsh climates and rough terrain.[1]

 Although the American English Coonhound has never placed at Westminster, the breed does well in a variety of coonhound events, obedience, agility, and course tests.[2]

 1995

Can He Tell by the Smell?

The American English Coonhound is a scent hound. They can follow a hot trail at a high rate of speed and find a cold trail with no problem. And once they're on to a scent, nothing and no one can hold them back. A Coonhound who is on the trail of something has a one-track mind—follow that smell!

Like other scent hounds, Coonhounds have especially sensitive noses. They can pick up smells humans can't. That means the smell is there, even if we can't detect it ourselves. Apparently, raccoon perfume is too much for a Coonhound to resist.

Actually, there are all kinds of smells in the air all the time. Some of them we can detect—like cookies baking or wet dog. And others are so faint we never notice them. And there are some that only God can smell.

Did you know that the Bible says *we* (believers) have a special smell to God? It does! We, who love God and choose to accept His son Jesus, are a pleasing smell to Him. Just as a Coonhound can pick up scents we can't,

Paws-itive Inspirations

God can tell those of us who are Christians just by our smell. Isn't that amazing? And what's more, He wants us to spread the aroma of the knowledge of Christ wherever we go. The more we do that, the more we create a pleasing fragrance for our heavenly Father to enjoy.

Consider this: Do our lives give off the pleasing smell of Jesus Christ to God? If we know Christ, and we do our best to live according to God's Word, we definitely do. Our goal in life should always be to make sure He can tell by the smell.

Unleash the Truth: "But thanks be to God, who always leads us as captives in Christ's triumphal procession and uses us to spread the aroma of the knowledge of him everywhere. For we are to God the pleasing aroma of Christ among those who are being saved and those who are perishing." (2 Corinthians 2:14–15)

Digging Deeper: What is it about your life that makes you different from a nonbeliever? Do you live your life so that your faith is obvious?

Fido 411: During a hunt, Coonhounds often chase their quarry right up a tree. They stay under the tree barking to alert their owners. But sometimes their prey manages to escape unnoticed. When that happens, the dogs are found to be "barking up the wrong tree." Today this phrase is a common American expression used to indicate someone is wrong about something.[3]

Weekly Tail-Waggers: Think about 2 Corinthians 2:14–15. Think about how you can spread the aroma of the knowledge of Christ everywhere you go. What are some ways you can do this? Treat others kindly. Always be truthful and fair. Help those who need help. Be a friend to others without expecting anything in return. Encourage others. Be ready to tell others about your faith when they ask. Be as much like Jesus as you can so that others will see Him in you.

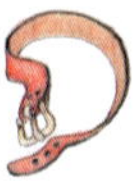

 Wendy

American Eskimo Dog

 Non-Sporting

 *Standard*—15 to 19 inches; 25 to 35 pounds, *Miniature*—12 to 15 inches; 10 to 20 pounds, *Toy*—9 to 12 inches; 6 to 10 pounds.

 Its name is quite confusing because the American Eskimo Dog or Eskie did not come from America. It is actually from Germany. It made its way to America by way of German immigrant families.

 Although a very beautiful breed, Eskies have never won Best in Show at Westminster. Inuk, an American Eskimo Dog, has won many awards in Canada and the United States, including Best of Breed at the 2019 Westminster Dog Show, but never won the top award.

 1994

God's Love Isn't Based on Your Performance

Eskies have been called the perfect combination of brains and beauty. They are smart and oh so pretty with that thick, shiny white coat. These beauties come from a long line of performers. In fact, these trick dogs used to perform and travel with various circuses in the late nineteenth century. The most famous Eskie, Pierre, actually walked a tightrope as part of the Barnum & Bailey Circus.[1] These show dogs loved the spotlight, and the spotlight loved them. With circuses mostly nonexistent today, these dogs are still performing, winning many agility awards in competitions across the country. Eskies perform well under pressure.

Do you perform well under pressure? Do you participate in a sport or an

Paws-itive Inspirations

art that puts you in front of crowds on a regular basis? Whether you're the best shooting guard on your basketball team or first-chair clarinet in your school's orchestra, your ability to perform under pressure is important. You start thinking, *If I don't practice hard and give it my all every time I'm called upon, I'll let everyone down.* It can be overwhelming if you only focus on winning the game or placing first in the orchestra competition. It's better to simply do your best and enjoy the task at hand. Take it from an Eskie.

That's why Eskies perform so well under pressure. See, they don't care if they win or lose; they simply love to do tricks, and they know their owners will love them whether or not they perform perfectly every time. Guess what—your heavenly Father won't love you any less if you miss the winning shot or forget your solo. He loves you no matter what. His love for you isn't based on your performance. His love is unconditional, so focus on that. Enjoy "the doing," and "the winning" will take care of itself.

 **Unleash the Truth:** "You were saved by faith in God, who treats us much better than we deserve. This is God's gift to you, and not anything you have done on your own." (Ephesians 2:8 CEV)

 **Digging Deeper:** Do you put too much pressure on yourself to perform perfectly all the time? That's a tough way to live. Give yourself a break today and remember that God loves you no matter what.

 Fido 411: Did you know the American Eskimo Dog used to be named the German Spitz but was renamed after World War I because so many people in America had bad feelings toward Germany? It's true.[2]

 Weekly Tail-Waggers: Find a way to encourage another "overachiever." If you see someone hurting because he missed an important shot or if you know your friend is sad that she didn't make first chair, take a moment to say something nice.

 *Michelle*

13

American Foxhound

 Hound

 21 to 25 inches; 40 to 66 pounds

 The American Foxhound descended from English, French, and, later, Irish hounds brought to the United States from Europe beginning in 1650.[1] George Washington was among the first to breed this true American hound—a taller, more athletic version of the European hounds.[2]

 The American Foxhound first appeared at Westminster in 1877. It has taken top honors in its group twice since then and placed an additional six times.[3]

 1886

Born to Bay

American Foxhounds are good-natured, easygoing hounds who get along well with children, dogs, and even cats! At first inspection, you might think the American Foxhound is perfect, but even this sweet breed has its flaws. In fact, American Foxhounds need lots of exercise or they can become depressed, and they have even been known to destroy stuff. Also, this independent breed can be challenging to housebreak and train for owners who aren't up for the challenge. And, if you live in town, next to a lot of other houses, the American Foxhound might not be the best dog for you if you want your neighbors to like you. Here's why—American Foxhounds are quite the singers ... or should I say howlers?[4]

They bay. Oh boy do they bay! Baying is like howling but is a term used exclusively for hounds. And this particular hound will bay every night,

Paws-itive Inspirations

especially if left alone. People who love this breed believe this special canine crooning is beautiful, but not everyone is a fan. That's why this dog is not recommended for those living in apartment buildings because they will bay loudly at night, and that is a very difficult thing to stop since it's part of who they are. You might say they were born to bay.

Guess what? So were you! Isaiah 12:5 says, "Sing praises to the Lord, for he has done gloriously; let this be made known in all the earth" (ESV). And Psalm 95:1 says, "Oh come, let us sing to the Lord; let us make a joyful noise to the rock of our salvation" (ESV). When God made us, He gave us the desire to praise Him. It's in us. We were born to praise, so go ahead and get your praise on! When you do, it not only blesses God, but also it brings you joy which strengthens you. (The Bible says that the joy of the Lord is our strength!) So the next time you feel that urge to break out in song and praise the Lord, go right ahead! Make a joyful noise because you were created to do so!

 **Unleash the Truth:** "Shout for joy to the Lord, all the earth. Worship the Lord with gladness; come before him with joyful songs." (Psalm 100:1-2)

 **Digging Deeper:** Did you know that you were created to praise God? Even if you don't always feel like giving God praise, do it anyway. The more you praise, the more you'll want to praise.

 Fido 411: The American Foxhound is closely associated with the states of Maryland and Virginia where the breed is believed to have originated. As a result, the state of Virginia adopted the American Foxhound as its state dog in 1966.[5]

 Weekly Tail-Waggers: This week, take time to praise God with song. You don't have to have a great singing voice. Even if your song sounds more like a hound dog's bay, God won't care. He will still think your song of praise is beautiful.

 Michelle

15

American Pit Bull Terrier

 Terrier

 17 to 19 inches; 40 to 70 pounds

 In the eighteenth and nineteenth centuries, many people in Great Britain entertained themselves by watching dog fights. These people bred strong, courageous dogs together to create the best possible fighting dogs, and the Pit Bull Terrier was born.

 Though American Pit Bull Terriers haven't won many awards in dog shows, an American Pit Bull Terrier named Stubby won the most war medals of any dog in World War I and was promoted to the rank of Sergeant.[1]

 1936

More than Meets the Eye

Since American Pit Bull Terriers were bred to fight, you'd think they would be pretty violent. And that has proven to be true in a few instances, but you can't judge an entire breed by a few highly publicized cases of pit bull attacks. Unfortunately, many people steer clear of adopting them for fear that they'll be dangerous and threatening to other animals and children. But here's something I bet you wouldn't guess: Pit Bull Terriers used to be nanny dogs because they were so gentle with children! That's right—despite their bad reputation, these dogs can actually be really big sweeties!

    We can judge other people in the same way that some people judge Pit Bull Terriers. We often think of people in a certain way because of things we've heard about them or because of one bad decision they've made. But

Paws-itive Inspirations

that's not the way God wants us to look at other people. He tells us to judge fairly, and that means giving everyone a chance!

Don't count somebody out before you know the whole story. Get to know that individual. Just because you've heard that someone is sort of a bully doesn't mean it's true. And just because you've seen a person do something that was questionable, that one incident shouldn't cancel out all of the good things that person has done. One mistake shouldn't define that person. You have to learn about a person for yourself in order to judge fairly! Just ask the Pit Bull Terrier—there's often a lot more than meets the eye!

 Unleash the Truth: "Speak up and judge fairly; defend the rights of the poor and needy." (Proverbs 31:9)

 Digging Deeper: Is there someone you have judged unfairly based on only a few things you know about that person? What might that person be like beyond what you've seen and heard? Why not give that person a chance to be your friend?

 **Fido 411:** When these powerful dogs were brought to America from Britain, the American breeders wanted their dogs to be heavier than their British cousins. They were renamed American Staffordshire Terriers because of the dogs' changes, but their nickname of "Pitbull" stuck with them.

 Weekly Tail-Waggers: This week, go out of your way to talk to someone you don't know very well. In your journal, write what surprised you most about that person. How would you describe that person now?

 *Michelle*

Australian Cattle Dog

   Herding

   17 to 20 inches; 35 to 50 pounds

   Australian Cattle Dogs were developed by Australian ranchers in the 1800s to help them on the range. The breed is a combination of Highland Collie, native wild dingoes, Dalmatian, and Kelpie.[1]

   Australian Cattle Dogs made their first appearance at Westminster in 1981. They haven't scored any wins there yet, but they do well in herding and agility trials.

   1980

A Life Well-Lived

Australian Cattle Dogs (ACDs) are sturdy and strong. They can run for long distances over rough terrain. And no matter how tired they are, they always seem to be able to put on a burst of speed when needed. Ranchers love them because they are smart and instinctively know how to work cattle.[2]

ACDs are also known for being long-lived. For almost one hundred years, an ACD named Bluey, held the Guinness World Record for living the longest of any known dog. Bluey was born in 1910. He worked for more than twenty years on his owner's ranch herding sheep and cattle. He died in November 1939, at the age of 29 years, 5 months, and 7 days.[3] Bluey's record wasn't broken until 2023![4]

Living a long and healthy life is a real blessing. Many people in the Bible who served God lived to be hundreds of years old. In fact, Methuselah lived to be 969 years old (Genesis 5:27)! Can you imagine?

Paws-itive Inspirations

But you know something? The blessing of a long, healthy life is actually a reward. The Bible commands us to honor our father and mother. To honor them is to obey them and treat them with respect. And the Bible also tells us that if we are faithful to do this, we will live a long life. It's the first commandment God gave that has a promise attached to it.

Obeying your parents might not seem like a big deal. There are lots of kids who don't. But if we want to be obedient to the Lord's command, and get a blessing besides, we need to do it—no matter how old we are.

Unleash the Truth: "Honor your father and mother. Then you will live a long, full life in the land the Lord your God is giving you." (Exodus 20:12 NLT)

"Children, obey your parents because you belong to the Lord, for this is the right thing to do." (Ephesians 6:1 NLT)

"Children, always obey your parents, for this pleases the Lord." (Colossians 3:20 NLT)

Digging Deeper: Have you ever disobeyed your parents?

Fido 411: Australian Cattle Dogs come in two colors. One is blue and the other is a red speckle. They are called Blue Heelers or Red Heelers depending on their color.[5]

Weekly Tail-Waggers: Make it a practice to obey your parents without arguing. For example, if they ask you to take out the garbage, do it cheerfully and don't put them off. Whenever you fall short of your obedience goal, be ready to admit it and ask forgiveness.

 *Wendy*

Australian Stumpy Tail Cattle Dog

 Herding

 17 to 20 inches; 32 to 45 pounds

 There are different opinions about this breed's beginnings but all agree it is from Australia. It is thought to be a descendent of the dingo, which was then bred with the Smithfield Collie, a black-and-white dog with a bobtail.[1]

 The Australian Stumpy Tail Cattle Dog has not won a Best in Show award at Westminster but the American Kennel Club honored a Stumpy named Betcha with a 2016 AKC Paw of Courage medal for his brave, dedicated service as a K-9 officer.[2]

  This breed was added to the AKC's Foundation Stock Service in 2018 in order to allow it to further develop and grow. The breeds on this list are not yet eligible for official AKC registration.

Beautifully Reliable

Often referred to as "the Stumpy," even the name of this breed lets you know that it's probably not the most attractive dog. It wasn't bred to be a beauty queen; it was bred to be a reliable cattle dog. With its strong build and speckled coat, this medium-sized dog is able to move cattle across long distances and over rough terrain and is able to survive extreme heat or cold. The Stumpy loves to be active and is happiest when it's herding something—cattle, sheep, and children. It's even been known to nip at grown-ups' heels in an attempt to herd them!

The Stumpy is the dog you want on the job because it won't stop until all of the work is done. While other breeds might get distracted, the Australian Stumpy Tail Cattle Dog stays focused on the task. It listens to its master's

Paws-itive Inspirations

commands and completes the work at hand. And, once that job is done, the Stumpy will joyfully return to its master, awaiting the next command.

How about you? Do you listen to your Master's commands and complete the work He has given you? For example, when God speaks to your heart with a gentle nudge to invite your friend to church, do you obey? Or, when your parents tell you to clean your room (and you know you should honor them because the Bible says you should), do you immediately start cleaning your room, or do you plop down on your bed and become distracted with your favorite video game?

Take a lesson from the Australian Stumpy Tail Cattle Dog—listen to your Master's commands, quickly obey, finish the work, and await your next assignment. If you do, you'll be a happy worker just like the Stumpy. Working for God has many rewards, including a supernatural joy in your heart. Become beautifully reliable today.

 Unleash the Truth: "The commandments of the Lord are right, bringing joy to the heart. The commands of the Lord are clear, giving insight for living." (Psalm 19:8 NLT)

 **Digging Deeper:** The Bible tells us in John 10:27 that if we are Christians, we can hear God's voice. Not in a big, booming way but right down in your heart. You'll have an urging to do what He instructs. When is the last time you "heard" God's voice?

 Fido 411: Did you know these dogs love the water and are great swimmers?

 **Weekly Tail-Waggers:** Practice makes perfect, right? Well, why don't you practice hearing God's voice? Grab your journal and have it nearby when you pray. Remember, prayer is a two-way communication between you and God. So, after you talk to Him, sit and listen. Do you feel God talking to your heart about anything? If so, write it down.

 *Michelle*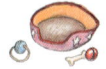

Basenji

(buh-SEN-jee)

 Hound

 16 to 17 inches; 22 to 24 pounds

 The Basenji is one of the oldest known breeds and is shown in Egyptian drawings going back to about 4,000 BC. It is originally from Central Africa.[1]

 The Basenji first appeared at Westminster in 1946. It took top honors in the Hound group in 1972 and has placed in ten other appearances.[2] Basenjis are eligible to compete in conformation, agility, rally, obedience, tracking, nose work, and lure coursing.[3]

 1944

We Walk by Faith

The Basenji is a hunter. Most dogs hunt by either sight or scent, but the Basenji uses both which makes them really good at it. In the bush country of Central Africa, packs of Basenjis were originally used by Pygmy tribes to drive prey into their waiting nets. The name Basenji means "dog of the bush."[4]

The Basenji relies on its sight and scent to find its way. As humans, we rely on our senses, especially sight and smell, to find our way around too. But when it comes to our faith walk, our human eyesight doesn't do us much good. Instead, the Bible says we are to walk by faith, not by sight.

The life of a believer isn't all rainbows and sunshine. Some days it's just hard. We live in a world full of sin and suffering. There are times when we give in to temptation and cause trouble for ourselves by our sin. Sometimes it isn't anything we do, but we are affected by some part of our sinful world. The main thing we have to remember is *whose* we are. We are children of God. We are made right with Him by our faith in Jesus Christ. By faith. That's important. If we are going to live the life God wants us to live and experience His peace and joy—it's going to take faith.

So what is faith? Faith is being sure of what you don't see and knowing (right down in your knower) that God is who He says He is, and that the only way to be happy is to live for Him. Living the Christian life isn't always easy. But the payoff is pretty spectacular. God rewards those who live by faith. Some rewards (like peace and joy) are for here and now. Other rewards we won't see until we get to heaven, but they will definitely be worth it. Walk by faith!

Unleash the Truth: "For we walk by faith, not by sight." (2 Corinthians 5:7 NKJV)

"We are made right with God by placing our faith in Jesus Christ. And this is true for everyone who believes, no matter who we are." (Romans 3:22 NLT)

"And it is impossible to please God without faith. Anyone who wants to come to him must believe that God exists and that he rewards those who sincerely seek him." (Hebrews 11:6 NLT)

Digging Deeper: How can you build your faith? (Hint: It's in the book!)

Fido 411: The Basenji is often called the "barkless" dog due to a flattened larynx. They are generally pretty quiet, but they can and *do* make noises. They whimper, whine, and growl just like other dogs. More interestingly, they produce a joyful yodel when happy and can emit a hair-raising scream when alarmed.[5]

Weekly Tail-Waggers: Hebrews 11 is known as the faith chapter. Take time to read it this week along with the first part of chapter 12. Be encouraged to walk by faith in your life, knowing that Jesus is waiting to welcome us at the finish line.

Wendy

Basset Hound

GROUP Hound

SIZE up to 15 inches, 40 to 65 pounds

ORIGIN Originally bred in France and Belgium, this low-to-the-ground breed became a popular hunting dog for French nobles.

Although Basset Hounds are a very popular breed, a Basset has never won the Westminster Dog Show.

AKC The American Kennel Club recognized the Basset Hound in 1885, making it the AKC's tenth breed.

Are You Loyal?

The first thing you'll notice about a Basset Hound is its droopy face and ears. Its appearance is pretty fitting for such a patient, easygoing pup! Even most cats love this breed because of its sweet and laid-back personality. Basset Hounds have powerful noses; their sense of smell is second only to the Bloodhound's. But there's one thing that Bassets are second-to-none at: they are fiercely loyal!

While many dog breeds are considered loyal, Basset Hounds have been deemed the most loyal of any breed, according to several experts in dog behavior. They are affectionate and like to be close to the people they love. They refuse to abandon their loved ones and will save them from danger if needed.

Loyalty is a great trait to have! Being loyal means others can count on you—no matter what! Loyal people believe the best about those they love, and they stick by them through good and bad times. Being loyal also means you're dependable, trustworthy, and committed. We want to model the Basset Hound and be a fiercely loyal friend to others and a devoted follower of God. Just like a Basset pup will stick by your side, show you lots of love, and protect you before themselves, you can show that kind of loyalty to the people in your life. (But probably without the droopy face and the slobber!)

Unleash the Truth: "And may your hearts be fully committed to the Lord our God, to live by his decrees and obey his commands, as at this time." (1 Kings 8:61)

Digging Deeper: Which people in your life do you consider loyal to you? Do you think you're a loyal person?

Fido 411: *Basset* is the French word for "low," so Basset Hound means, "a hound that is low to the ground"!

Weekly Tail-Waggers: In your journal, make a list of things you think a loyal person might do. How many of those things can you do for others and for God this week?

Michelle

Beagle

Group Hound

Size under 15 inches; under 30 pounds

Origin The Beagle's ancestors possibly go back to 400 BC in Greece where they were used to hunt rabbits. By the 1700s rabbit hunting with packs of Beagles was a popular sport in Europe.[1]

Beagles were originally considered sporting dogs. Later classified as hounds, Beagles have taken Best in Show two times at Westminster. They have placed in their group (Sporting and Hound) a total of thirty-eight times.[2]

AKC 1885

The Greatest Friend of All

Beagles are scent hounds. Their nose knows, and that makes them a natural for tracking and nose work. They have a real talent for sniffing out things like termites, food being smuggled in through airports, drugs, explosives, and bedbugs. They are even used to locate pregnant polar bears! (Yes, they really can tell which ones are pregnant. They can tell by the, uh, poop.)[3]

But the Beagle's noble nose isn't their only winning quality. A friendly personality makes them great therapy dogs too. They make the perfect friend to cuddle up with when life is hard. Beagles are also great at making friends.[4]

Making friends isn't always easy. For some people it's really hard. But *being* a friend is something else. Being a friend is doing what a Beagle does and being there for someone else. Even if you're a shy person, you can show friendship to others by being kind and treating them the way you would like to be treated. The chances are good that if you treat others kindly, they'll see you as a friend.

But more important than our earthly friendships is our friendship with God. When we become believers and accept Jesus Christ as Lord and Savior, we become a friend of God—the creator of the universe! Talk about friends in high places! The best part: God is, and always will be, the best friend we could ever have. People may let you down. But God is a friend who is always there for you. He loves you more than your mom or your dad or your brother. He even loves you more than your grandma! And He will never leave you or abandon you. He always listens. He knows what you need before you know yourself. And He answers every prayer. Always. Now *that's* a friend worth having.

Unleash the Truth: "Friendship with God is reserved for those who reverence him. With them alone he shares the secrets of his promises." (Psalm 25:14 TLB)

"So now we can rejoice in our wonderful new relationship with God because our Lord Jesus Christ has made us friends of God." (Romans 5:11 NLT)

"A man who has friends must himself be friendly, But there is a friend who sticks closer than a brother." (Proverbs 18:24 NKJV)

Digging Deeper: Has a friend ever let you down?

Fido 411: The Beagle's white tipped tail is no accident. They are bred this way to make them easier to spot while hunting.[5]

Weekly Tail-Waggers: This week think about ways you can be a friend to others. You can offer to help someone with their homework. You can sit with someone who doesn't have anyone to sit with at lunch. Or you might just listen to someone who needs to talk. And while you're being a friend to someone else, you can thank God that He is the best friend you will ever have.

Wendy

Bearded Collie

GROUP Herding

SIZE 20 to 22 inches; 40 to 55 pounds

ORIGIN Bearded Collies, or Beardies, have been found in art dating back to the 1700s. It's believed they are a result of crossing English Sheepdogs and Collies.[1]

Sophie, a three-year-old Bearded Collie, won Best of Opposite at her very first Westminster in 2022, but it's no surprise. Her father, Dunhill Steelers Nation, won Best of Breed in 2017. (Best of Opposite is given to the dog who is the opposite sex of the Best of Breed Winner.) Also, the Bearded Collie won the Herding Group in 1996 and 2011.[2]

AKC 1976

Mistaken Identity

I remember the first time I heard the name "Bearded Collie" I immediately thought of the famous Lassie dog with a beard, lol. Well, that definitely isn't what a Bearded Collie looks like. In fact, Bearded Collies are often mistaken for Old English Sheepdogs because they look more like a Sheepdog than a Collie.

Has that ever happened to you? Have you ever been mistaken for someone else? It happens to me all the time. People will approach me at airports or theme parks and then become embarrassed when I'm not who they thought I was. They'll say things like, "Wow, I can't believe you're not her! She could be your twin!" I always respond, "I guess I just have one of those faces." It really does happen quite often.

But you know who never mistakes me for anyone else? God.

No matter if I change my hair color. Lose weight. Gain weight. Wear a disguise. God always knows who I am, and He always knows who you are too. You see, God made us. He knows every hair on our heads. And, the Bible says that even though people look at our outward appearance, God looks at our hearts. That means He really knows us, and that is comforting, isn't it? God knows our insides and our outsides. He knows the good, the bad, and the ugly about us, and He still loves us.

Unleash the Truth: "Why, even the hairs of your head are all numbered." (Luke 12:7 ESV)

Digging Deeper: Do you ever feel "unknown" or like nobody really knows you? Well, your heavenly Father knows you, and He adores you. Never worry about trying to hide your true self from God. He knows the real you, and He loves you more than you can ever imagine.

Fido 411: Bearded Collies have a very unique double coat. The outer coat is long, thick, and quite shaggy. But their undercoat is soft and warm. This combination not only provides an adorable scruffy look but also gives these dogs protection from the cold.

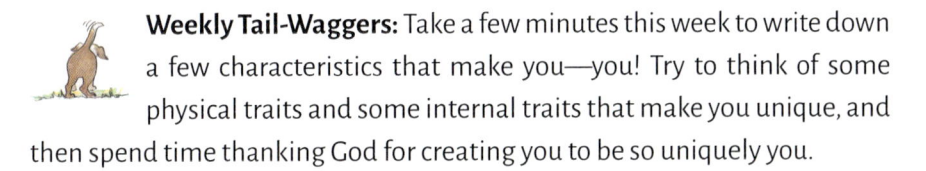

Weekly Tail-Waggers: Take a few minutes this week to write down a few characteristics that make you—you! Try to think of some physical traits and some internal traits that make you unique, and then spend time thanking God for creating you to be so uniquely you.

Michelle

Belgian Malinois
(MA-lun-wah)

GROUP Herding

SIZE 22 to 26 inches; 40 to 80 pounds

ORIGIN These dogs were first bred in Malines, Belgium, as companions for shepherds and cattlemen. They were brought to America in 1911 and now serve as great police and military dogs.

This breed has never won Best in Show at Westminster. But, a Belgian Malinois named Pablo was one of five winners of the American Kennel Club Humane Fund Awards for Canine Excellence in 2015. Now retired, Pablo was certified by the US Air Force as a Patrol/Explosive Detection Dog. He has also served in protecting several United States presidents and even regularly attended church with former president Jimmy Carter to protect him while he taught Bible study.[1]

AKC 1959

What's Your Passion?

Belgian Malinois are smart, confident, strong, and hardworking, which make them great police and military dogs. But what makes them truly excellent working dogs is their unbreakable bond with their human partners. They are eager to please their masters and never want to leave their side.

When Malinois don't have a job to do, they can get depressed. They need lots of exercise and plenty of time with their beloved owners. To deny a Malinois activity and the pleasure of your company is to deprive him of his very reasons for living. Without a job from their adored master, these dogs feel lost and alone. It brings them great joy to serve their masters.

We can be a lot like Malinois in this way. We have an unbreakable bond with our own Master in heaven. And, when we don't spend enough time with Him, we can feel depressed and lose our reason for living. Like this very special breed, we need to be passionate about serving God (our Master) and find a way to spend plenty of time with Him! If we do those things, we will have so much joy in our hearts that if we had tails, they'd be wagging.

Unleash the Truth: "I open my mouth and pant, longing for your commands." (Psalm 119:131)

Digging Deeper: What are some things that you feel deeply passionate about? How can you create that same amount of passion for God?

Fido 411: Because of their history as herding dogs, Malinois are fierce protectors of farms and families.

Weekly Tail-Waggers: Create a time in your daily schedule to spend at least ten minutes with God. Use that time to pray, read the Bible, or sing along to worship music. Try your best to fit those ten minutes into every day this week.

Michelle

Bernese Mountain Dog

GROUP Working

SIZE 23 to 27.5 inches; 70 to 115 pounds

ORIGIN The Bernese Mountain Dog (BMD) originated in the Bern area of Switzerland as an all-purpose farm dog.[1]

The BMD has taken the top spot in the Working group twice at Westminster since 1943.[2] BMDs also compete in conformation, obedience, rally, drafting, tracking, herding, agility, and therapy work.[3] The Bernese Mountain Dog Club of America offers special awards to BMDs including one for Grand Master Draft Dog. The Grand Master Draft Dog title is awarded to dogs who complete the requirements for eight draft titles.[4]

AKC 1937

Carrying the Load

A BMD is a great example of a really good dog. They are affectionate, intelligent, loyal, and faithful. And, boy, can they work! BMDs herd cattle, make good watchdogs, and are excellent draft dogs. A draft dog is one that can carry or pull heavy loads. Many years ago in Switzerland, where this breed originated, farmers who couldn't afford a horse used large dogs like a BMD to pull carts and other loads.[5]

For the BMD, pulling a heavy load for his people is a joy. They love to help their humans. But, for people, carrying a heavy load is anything *but* a joy. It's hard. Often, the loads we carry aren't physical ones. For us, the loads are more like the stress that comes from school, the heartbreak of having parents divorce, or the trauma of being betrayed by a friend. When we try to carry things like that around with us, we can become tired and depressed. Sometimes the load is just too heavy.

Jesus knew all about the loads we would have to carry in our lives. And He wants us to know He's here to help. That's why He tells us to come to Him. In the book of Matthew, Jesus tells us to take His yoke upon us. A yoke is a collar that goes on an animal. The collar attaches the animal to a cart or plow and allows it to pull the load. Often the yoke is designed for two. Jesus is inviting us to be yoked with Him in life. When we pull together, Jesus will help us carry our load. In fact, He promises to carry most of the weight to give us rest. With Jesus, the burden, no matter what it may be, is easier. And just like the BMD, Jesus takes great joy in carrying our load.

Unleash the Truth: "Come to me, all you who are weary and burdened, and I will give you rest. Take my yoke upon you and learn from me, for I am gentle and humble in heart, and you will find rest for your souls. For my yoke is easy and my burden is light." (Matthew 11:28–30)

Digging Deeper: Are there any burdens or loads in your life that you are trying to carry by yourself?

Fido 411: In Switzerland, BMDs were used to transport milk and cheese from the mountains to the valleys below. The Swiss sometimes referred to them as Cheese Dogs.[6]

Weekly Tail-Waggers: If you are struggling with some burdens by yourself, ask Jesus to help you. Give all your cares to Him because He loves you and wants to lighten your load.

Wendy

Bichon Frise
(bee-SHAAN free-ZAY)

Group Non-Sporting

Size 9.5 to 11.5 inches; 11 to 15 pounds

Origin Bichon Frises originated in the Mediterranean regions and were often taken along on sea voyages by Spanish and Italian sailors. In the 1500s they were the favorite dog of French royalty. Bichons first appeared in the United States in 1956 and have become a popular companion dog.[1]

Bichons are crowd pleasers in any competition. They have taken top honors (Best in Show) at Westminster twice since their first appearance there in 1974. The most recent was in 2018.[2] Bichons also excel in agility competitions.[3]

AKC 1973

To Make Friends, Be a Friend

The name Bichon Frise means "small dog with curly hair" or "fluffy little dog." Their dense undercoat and curly outer coat make them look like a white powder puff—one that walks and barks.[4] They're cute as a button, for sure, but that's not what makes them so popular.

The Bichon's signature trait is its cheerful personality and friendly disposition. They easily win friends with their expressive eyes and strong desire to make people smile. To them, there are no strangers, just friends they haven't met yet. Because they approach others with such friendliness, they are usually met with smiles and "scritches" wherever they go.[5]

The Bible says having friends is a good thing. But to have friends, you first have to be friendly toward others. Like the Bichon, you have to approach people with a smile and a desire to put them at ease. Does that work on everyone all the time? No. But then, you never know what's going on in someone else's head. In general, though, when you are friendly toward others, you'll get a positive response.

Unleash the Truth: "A man who has friends must himself be friendly." (Proverbs 18:24a NKJV)

"The seeds of good deeds become a tree of life; a wise person wins friends." (Proverbs 11:30 NLT)

Digging Deeper: Think about how you meet new people or interact with others. Do you smile? Do you listen more than you talk? Do you offer to help when you can? Do you make eye contact? Do you think the way you meet or greet others is positive or negative?

Fido 411: Bichon's love to run, which makes them a natural for agility competitions. They can tear through an agility course at surprising speeds. They're fun to watch because they have such fun doing it.

Weekly Tail-Waggers: If you have trouble making friends, first take it to the Lord. Ask God to help you make and be a friend. Even if you are very shy, you can go through your day with a smile on your face. You'll be surprised at how others will respond to you.

Wendy

Bloodhound

Group: Hound

Size: 23 to 27 inches; 80 to 110 pounds

Origin: The Bloodhounds we know and love today were first bred by Western European church officials one thousand years ago. In fact, whole packs of hounds were kept in monasteries in England and France.

Toot My Own Horn became the first Bloodhound to ever win Best of Show at the prestigious Westminster Dog Show in 2022. A Bloodhound also won the AKC Championship in 2005. A Bloodhound named Inspector Gadget won the 2018 American Kennel Club Humane Fund Award for Canine Excellence. He is a search-and-rescue dog and has assisted in locating dozens of missing persons and bringing them home.[1] How cool is that!

AKC: 1885

Super Sleuths

This world-famous "Sleuth Hound" does one thing better than any other creature on earth: finds people who are lost or hiding. The Bloodhound has the strongest, most reliable sense of smell of any dog breed. That's why many of them work with detective agencies and police forces to help locate missing people.

When off duty, the Bloodhound is one of the canine kingdom's calmest citizens. But once he catches a scent, he can be relentless and stubborn until he locates the source of that scent. In fact, training a Bloodhound to be an obedient pet can be challenging because Bloodhounds love following their noses, not directions. When taking a Bloodhound on a walk, you have to have a strong leash and a strong will to keep him from following all of the new scents bombarding him.

Because of their drive to follow smells, Bloodhounds love their jobs of searching for lost people. They will pursue a scent with determination for hours, even days if needed. In Matthew 18:22, the Bible says that God will pursue us when we're lost. The kind of "lost" the Bible is talking about here means those who aren't living for God. Even though there are billions of people in the world, God loves each one of us so much that if even one of us wanders away from Him, He will track us down so He can bring us back to Him and His unconditional love. And, God is even better at finding us than a sniffing Bloodhound!

Unleash the Truth: "If a man has a hundred sheep and one of them wanders away, what will he do? Won't he leave the ninety-nine others on the hills and go out to search for the one that is lost? And if he finds it, I tell you the truth, he will rejoice over it more than over the ninety-nine that didn't wander away!" (Matthew 18:12–13 NLT)

Digging Deeper: Have there been times in your life when you wandered away from God? Did you know that God was constantly trying to rescue you and bring you home to Him?

Fido 411: A Bloodhound's nose is so reliable that almost any court will accept the results of a Bloodhound's tracking as evidence!

Weekly Tail-Waggers: Let's say a prayer and thank God for His love and ask Him for His guidance, and let's also pray for the people who are still lost.

Father God, I want to thank You for loving me, no matter what. Thank You, God, for pursuing me when I didn't follow You, and thank You for never giving up on me. I pray right now for _____ [insert the names of your friends or family members who don't know God] that You will find them, that You will rescue them, and that they will follow You. In Your Son's mighty name, amen.

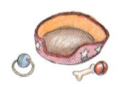

Michelle

Border Collie

Group: Herding

Size: 18 to 22 inches; 30 to 55 pounds

Origin: Border Collies, whose ancestors were ancient Roman and Viking herd dogs, made a name for themselves in the rocky highlands of Scotland and Wales.[1]

Border Collies have taken top honors in the Westminster agility contest all but one year since it began in 2014.[2]

AKC: 1995

Obedience Counts

Border Collies are hardworking dogs who love having a job to do. A Border Collie who isn't working is NOT a happy camper. They're super smart and always keep a close eye on their owner for instructions and directions. In fact, they're known for their intense gaze known as "the eye."[3]

When working with a Border Collie, the owner uses voice commands, whistles, and hand signals. The Borders watch and listen carefully to round up sheep or other animals, move them from pasture to pasture, or separate a single animal from the herd. It's absolutely amazing to watch! Their skill and instant obedience make a shepherd's job much easier.[4]

Obedience to its master is a desirable trait in a Border Collie. But they're not the only ones. God desires that trait in us too. He loves us no matter what. But if we really want to please Him and prove our love for Him, we will obey Him. And we'll listen carefully when He speaks to us so that we can obey His directions immediately.

Unleash the Truth: "If you love me, obey my commandments." (John 14:15 NLT)

"My sheep listen to my voice; I know them, and they follow me." (John 10:27 NLT)

Digging Deeper: Can you remember a time when you disobeyed someone who had proper authority over you? How did it make you feel? Did it change how the person you disobeyed treated you?

Fido 411: Most Border Collies are descended from a dog named Old Hemp. He was born in Northern England in 1894. He was such a great dog that many farmers wanted pups fathered by him. As a result, Old Hemp sired more than two hundred pups.[5]

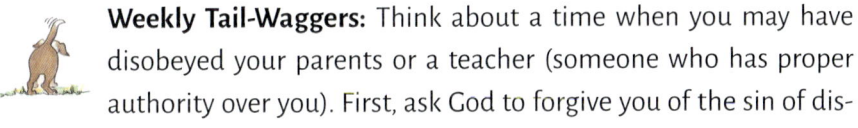

Weekly Tail-Waggers: Think about a time when you may have disobeyed your parents or a teacher (someone who has proper authority over you). First, ask God to forgive you of the sin of disobedience. Then, go to the person you disobeyed. Ask their forgiveness and make it right if you can. You'll feel better, and it will go a long way toward improving your relationship.

Wendy

Boston Terrier

GROUP Non-Sporting

SIZE 15 to 17 inches; 12 to 25 pounds

ORIGIN This breed began in the United States. It is a cross between an English Terrier and a Bulldog. It was first named the American Bull Terrier but later changed to the Boston Terrier to honor the city of Boston, Massachusetts.

The Boston Terrier has never won Best in Show, but in 1921 General John Pershing awarded the Humane Education Society Gold Medal to a war dog named Sergeant Stubby, who probably came from this breed.[1]

AKC 1893

Names Matter

Nicknamed the "American Gentleman" because of its tuxedo-like markings, the Boston Terrier has quite an interesting history. In 1889, a group who loved this black-and-white little dog got together and began the American Bull Terrier Club, which made sense at the time, because these dogs were called bull terriers or round heads. However, this new club received some negative feedback about its name choice because a very different kind of dog with a much longer snout and face had already claimed the breed name "bull terrier." So, in 1891 the club officially changed its name to the Boston Terrier Club and no one called the adorable little dogs round heads or bull terriers ever again.[2]

Names are important. In the Bible, God often changed people's names when they had a change of heart or circumstance. For example, He changed Sarai, which means "my princess," to Sarah, which means "mother of nations," after she became pregnant with her son, Isaac. And, God changed Abram's name, which means "high father," to Abraham, which means "father of a multitude," because that was his destiny. He also changed Jacob's name, which means "the deceiver," to Israel, which means "one who has prevailed with God."

Do you know what your name means? If not, ask an adult to help you learn the meaning of your name. For example, Michelle means "Godly woman" and Wendy means "friend." But, no matter what your given name means, God has another name for you—child of God! And unlike the Boston Terrier, which was originally named the Bull Terrier, no one can take or change your name—child of God. It's yours! Believe it, celebrate it, and walk a little taller today, knowing *who* you are and *whose* you are.

Unleash the Truth: "But now, thus says the Lord, who created you, O Jacob, And He who formed you, O Israel: 'Fear not, for I have redeemed you; I have called *you* by your name; You *are* Mine.'" (Isaiah 43:1 NKJV)

Digging Deeper: Have you ever wanted a different name? What name would you choose, if you could change your name, and why?

Fido 411: Did you know the Boston Terrier is the official mascot of Boston University? And, in 1979 the Boston Terrier was named the official state dog of Massachusetts.[3]

Weekly Tail-Waggers: The Bible tells us about many names that God calls His children. For example, it says in 2 Corinthians 5:17, that God calls us a new creature! (Because once we give our lives to Him, that's what we become—new creatures!) See if you can find a few other names that God calls you by studying the Bible this week or by using a Bible website.

Michelle

Boxer

GROUP — Working

SIZE — 21.5 to 25 inches; 50 to 80 pounds

ORIGIN — The Boxer's ancestors go all the way back to Assyrian war dogs in 2500 BC, but the Boxer we know today was developed in the late 1800s by breeders in Germany.[1]

The Boxer is often a winner in a big way at Westminster. Boxers have taken Best in Show four times and have won first place in their Working group an impressive twenty-six times![2]

AKC — 1904

A Merry Heart

A Boxer is a medium-sized, square-built dog. They are strong and fast and have amazing endurance. When on guard, the Boxer is alert, dignified, and sure of himself. One thing is for sure, they are the last thing an intruder or burglar ever wants to see. When it comes to protecting those they love, Boxers are all business.

But underneath all that dignified alertness beats the heart of a clown. When it's playtime, Boxers are real goofballs. They love to play and act silly. And they take great delight in making everyone laugh. Somehow, they know. There's a time for work and a time for silliness. And Boxers are great at both.[3]

How about you? Are you all business when it comes to work? And do you enjoy laughing and cutting up a little when the work is done? Work and school are good, but so is a sense of humor and laughter. We need both to be

Paws-itive Inspirations

happy and balanced. If one of those things takes up too much of our time, we can get out of balance. That can lead to stress and feeling overwhelmed or depressed.

The Bible tells us how to live so that we can be healthy and happy. Our work, whether it's school or a job or good deeds, is important. But it's also important to laugh a little too. Laughter strengthens our immune system, improves our mood, decreases pain, and helps with stress. Scientists say it can positively affect our health in lots of ways.[4] It really is good medicine.

Unleash the Truth: "A cheerful heart is good medicine, but a crushed spirit dries up the bones." (Proverbs 17:22)

"There is a time for everything, and a season for every activity under the heavens: . . . a time to weep and a time to laugh, a time to mourn and a time to dance." (Ecclesiastes 3:1, 4)

Digging Deeper: What makes you laugh?

Fido 411: Boxers love their toys. And not just as puppies. They keep and play with their favorite toys even in their old age.[5]

Weekly Tail-Waggers: School (with all that homework and testing and those sticky social situations) can be pretty stressful. Add in the other activities you might be involved with, and you just might find yourself getting all stressed out. Make time this week to laugh a little. It'll do you good.

Wendy

Bull Terrier

GROUP   Terrier

SIZE   21 to 22 inches; 50 to 70 pounds

ORIGIN   The Bull Terrier, a cross between an English Bulldog and various terriers, was bred in England in the early 1800s. It was intended to be a pit fighter but was never vicious enough. Pit fighting is now illegal, but the Bull Terrier has become a favorite companion dog due to its friendly and affectionate nature.[1]

Colored Bull Terriers (any color other than white with or without white markings) and White Bull Terriers are shown as separate varieties of the same breed. Both varieties first appeared at Westminster in 1877. Both have taken a Best in Show award—the most recent being a red Bull Terrier in 2006.[2]

AKC   1885

You Are the Only You There Is—And You Are Amazing

The Bull Terrier is a solid dog with an athletic build. They're fun-loving and make great family dogs. But they are best known for their long egg-shaped faces and Roman noses. Oh, and one other thing. Bull Terriers have another physical characteristic you won't see in any other registered dog. They have triangular-shaped eyes. They really are unique.

Scientists tell us no two human beings are exactly alike. We don't have triangular-shaped eyes, but each of us is different. The Bible tells us we are fearfully and wonderfully made by God and that He knew us before the world began. We are all human. We are all composed of the same materials. But we are all different. We are all amazingly unique.[3]

That means there's only one you! You are who you are because God planned it that way. He needed a you. He has a plan and purpose just for you. No one else can fulfill that plan but you. The Bible says our whole lives were recorded in God's book before we ever took our first breath. We're His masterpiece! And we were created to do the things He planned for us before the world began. Take comfort and joy in that thought. When you're feeling as though you don't matter or that no one sees you, remember this: God created you to be who you are. You are uniquely you. And no one else can do you like *you*.

Unleash the Truth: "For you created my inmost being; you knit me together in my mother's womb. I praise you because I am fearfully and wonderfully made; your works are wonderful, I know that full well." (Psalm 139: 13–14)

"You saw me before I was born. Every day of my life was recorded in your book. Every moment was laid out before a single day had passed." (Psalm 139:16 NLT)

"For we are God's masterpiece. He has created us anew in Christ Jesus, so we can do the good things he planned for us long ago." (Ephesians 2:10 NLT)

Digging Deeper: Do you ever feel as though you are unnoticed or unappreciated?

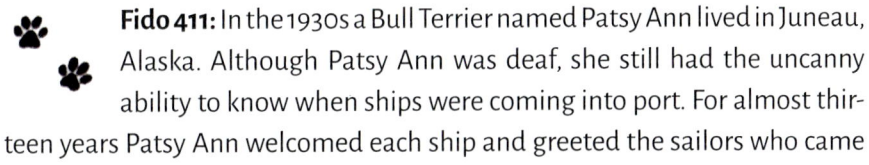

Fido 411: In the 1930s a Bull Terrier named Patsy Ann lived in Juneau, Alaska. Although Patsy Ann was deaf, she still had the uncanny ability to know when ships were coming into port. For almost thirteen years Patsy Ann welcomed each ship and greeted the sailors who came ashore. She was also careful to spread her special brand of cheerful friendship among the locals. When she died, a statue was erected in her honor.[4]

Weekly Tail-Waggers: This week read Psalm 139. Think about all the ways God has created *you* to be just the way you are.

Wendy

Bulldog

GROUP — Non-Sporting

SIZE — 14 to 15 inches; 40 to 50 pounds

ORIGIN — Bulldogs originated in England and may go back as far as eight hundred years. They were originally bred to guard, control, and bait bulls but haven't been used for that purpose since 1835.[1]

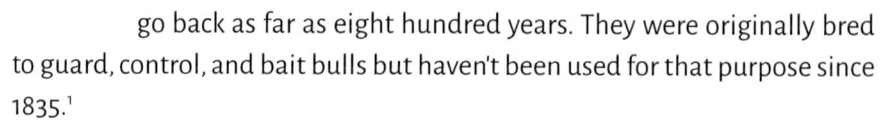

Bulldogs have taken the top spot at Westminster twice in their long history there and have placed in their group many times.[2] In 2019, a Bulldog named Thor won Best in Show at the US National Dog Show.[3]

AKC — 1886

Never Give Up

Bulldogs are massive, powerful dogs that travel low to the ground. They have a large head with a lower jaw that sticks out from a flat muzzle. This combination doesn't make for a beautiful dog, but it does allow the Bulldog to get a grip on something and not let go. They never give up.

During World War I, the Bulldog became a national mascot to England. By the time that war ended, most of the world associated Bulldogs with the English. Like the Bulldog, they never gave up.

During World War II, Prime Minister Winston Churchill (who looked a bit like a Bulldog himself) encouraged his people to stand firm. In one speech he said, "never give in, never give in, never, never, never, never—in nothing, great or small, large or petty—never give in except to convictions of honour and good sense."[4]

Sometimes it's hard to hang in there. It's hard to study for that math test,

Paws-itive Inspirations

especially if math isn't your best subject. It can be hard to keep practicing for a sport if you're not winning. Sometimes it's hard to keep working on badges for your scouting group when you'd rather be doing something else. It can be even harder to follow through on a promise to do a good deed—like helping the neighbor mow their lawn.

We all have situations in life where we'd like to just forget it and move on. Sometimes the things we would like to quit aren't all that hard, we just don't want to do them anymore. And sometimes the things we want to quit are good things; it's just that we're tired of doing them. It happens to everyone.

But the Bible tells us that *everything* a believer does is important. That's because whatever we do is for God's glory. He wants us to treat every job or task we do as though it was especially for Him. When the task is hard, don't give up. When the job is boring, don't give up. Whatever you do, do it for the glory of God. And *never* give up.

Unleash the Truth: "Whatever you do, work at it with all your heart, as working for the Lord, not for human masters." (Colossians 3:23)

"Let us not become weary in doing good, for at the proper time we will reap a harvest if we do not give up." (Galatians 6:9)

Digging Deeper: Have you ever wanted to give up on something or someone?

Fido 411: In spite of their size and shape, Bulldogs are really good at a variety of sports. For example, a Bulldog in Lima, Peru, named Otto, holds the Guinness World Record for traveling through a human tunnel on a skateboard. Otto skated through the legs of thirty people to win the world record.[5]

Weekly Tail-Waggers: Is there something in your life that you've thought about quitting? Think carefully about whatever that is. Is it honorable? Is it a good thing to do? If the answer is yes, make a commitment to yourself that you will not give up until your task is done.

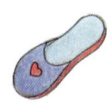

Wendy

Bullmastiff

GROUP Working

SIZE 24 to 27 inches; 100 to 130 pounds

ORIGIN English gamekeepers created the Bullmastiff in the mid-1800s to guard against poachers. The breed is a cross between the Bulldog and an Old English Mastiff.[1]

The Bullmastiff took first place in the Working group in 1992 at Westminster and has placed on four other occasions.[2] Bullmastiffs can compete in agility, rally, and obedience competitions, but their stubbornness sometimes makes these events a challenge for them.[3]

AKC 1934

Heads Up!

The original Bullmastiff was known as the "Gamekeeper's Night Dog." The perfect blend of power and speed, the Bullmastiff was especially bred to blend in with the night and the underbrush. They were meant to roam the estate grounds patrolling for poachers. Their job was to sneak up on an intruder or poacher, take him down, and hold him until the gamekeeper arrived on the scene. Once the dog had the poacher under control, there was no getting away. They were caught.[4]

Unfortunately, all believers have an enemy. God's enemy, Satan, is also our enemy. The Bible warns us that he is always on the prowl looking for those he can destroy. He's always looking for an opportunity to catch us with our guard down. He wants to sneak up on us when we least suspect it. And just like those poachers caught by a Bullmastiff, once we're caught, we're in for a bad time.

Paws-itive Inspirations

But here's something to think about: those poachers were somewhere they weren't supposed to be, doing something they weren't supposed to be doing. If they hadn't been there, there would have been no reason to fear the gamekeeper's dog. Instead, they were caught and severely punished.

When we are obedient to God and are busy doing the good things He has shown us in His Word, we're not likely to be caught off guard. We don't have to fear our enemy because we know the One (Jesus) who is in us is greater. When we pray and read our Bibles on a regular basis, we become more alert to things that are not of God. Satan may try to tempt us or cause us to stumble, but we have the power to resist him and make him run. It's our job to be aware of his tricks and to submit ourselves to God so we can be well-equipped to overcome our enemy.

Unleash the Truth: "Stay alert! Watch out for your great enemy, the devil. He prowls around like a roaring lion, looking for someone to devour." (1 Peter 5:8 NLT)

"You are of God, little children, and have overcome them, because He who is in you is greater than he who is in the world." (1 John 4:4 NKJV)

"Submit yourselves, then, to God. Resist the devil, and he will flee from you." (James 4:7)

Digging Deeper: How does the enemy tempt us? Do you think it's the same for everyone? How did the enemy tempt Jesus?

Fido 411: Although early Bullmastiffs were dark in color, today's dogs are often fawn colored (a light, yellowish tan) to highlight their Mastiff ancestry.[5]

Weekly Tail-Waggers: Take a moment to read about the temptation of Jesus this week (Matthew 4:1–11). Notice that Jesus used the Word to resist Satan. The Word is our weapon too (Ephesians 6:17).

Wendy

49

Cairn Terrier

GROUP Terrier

SIZE 9.5 to 10 inches; 13 to 14 pounds

ORIGIN Cairn Terriers go back as far as the 1600s and were originally known as "earth dogges." Their specialty was hunting the vermin that lived among the cairns (the stone piles that served as memorials or landmarks throughout the Scottish Highlands).[1]

Cairn Terriers took top honors among the Terrier group in 1988 at Westminster; however, they have never been awarded Best in Show. Cairns are highly adaptable and excel in a variety of competitive activities.[2]

AKC 1913

Think Before You Speak

Cairn Terriers are small, scrappy dogs who are basically fearless. They don't back up from anything. And because of their heritage they have a tendency to chase anything that moves. Anything. Without a thought. If it moves, they're on it. And that can lead to trouble.

There are some things that aren't supposed to be chased: babies, little old ladies, the cat, the neighbor's Rottweiler, and more. Chasing any of those things (including those in the "more" category) could cause harm to the chaser or chasee. It takes training and an owner with a strong personality to help the Cairn overcome the urge to chase. But in the end, well-behaved Cairns are happier and a lot less likely to get themselves in a pickle.

For humans, the hardest thing to control is the urge to talk. That's because, just like Cairns chase without thought, we humans can speak without thought. And the words we speak can cause pain for others, or they can get us into trouble.

It happens. At one time or another everyone says something without thinking—and then immediately regrets it. They wish they could take it back. But that's the thing about our words: once we say them, we can't take them back. If the words cause damage, we can't undo the damage. That's why it's so important to think before we speak. We need to make sure that the words that come out of our mouths will build others up and glorify God.

You've heard and maybe even said, "Sticks and stones may break my bones, but words will never hurt me." There's just one problem with that saying. It isn't true. Words can hurt every bit as much as sticks and stones. Sometimes words can leave wounds that *never* heal.

A wise person puts a guard on his or her mouth. How? That person asks the Holy Spirit to direct his or her thoughts and words so that they are always pleasing to God.

Unleash the Truth: "Those who guard their lips preserve their lives, but those who speak rashly will come to ruin." (Proverbs 13:3)

"Those who consider themselves religious and yet do not keep a tight rein on their tongues deceive themselves, and their religion is worthless." (James 1:26)

Digging Deeper: Have you ever said something without thinking that hurt someone or caused you to get in trouble?

Fido 411: Cairn Terriers are sometimes called Toto dogs. They got the nickname from MGM's 1939 movie *The Wizard of Oz*, which starred a female brindle-colored Cairn named Terry.[3]

Weekly Tail-Waggers: Spend some time this week thinking about your words. Do they build others up, or do they tear them down? Commit to making sure your words are truthful and carefully considered before they are spoken. Pray this prayer from Psalm 19:14: "Let the words of my mouth and the meditation of my heart Be acceptable in Your sight, O Lord, my strength and my Redeemer" (NKJV). Amen.

Wendy

Cane Corso

GROUP Working

SIZE 24 to 27 inches; 88 to 110 pounds

ORIGIN The Corso dates back to ancient Roman times. Bred as protectors, their name, translated from Latin, means "bodyguard dog."[1] The first Corso showed up in the United States in 1988.

Only four Corsos in the history of the AKC have won Best in Show.

AKC 2010

You Are Chosen

Originally bred to hunt wild boars and serve as watchdogs, Cane Corsos are big, protective, intimidating dogs. But they have also been called gentle giants because they make wonderful emotional support animals. In fact, a nonprofit organization called Corsos for Heroes provides dogs for disabled veterans and first responders who have experienced trauma, and these dogs are making a big difference.

Interesting, isn't it? A big, intimidating dog whose very presence can seem scary—not to mention its intense bark—is also the same dog that brings such comfort and peace to its owners. If you were going to choose a comfort animal, a Corso probably wouldn't be the first breed that would come to mind. Yet, Corsos are amazing at offering emotional support. It's a good reminder that God can use us in a big way, even if the world counts us out. Even if we aren't the obvious choice.

There are lots of examples of this in the Bible. Take Moses, for instance. By the time God called Moses to deliver His people from Egypt, he was already eighty years old. And the Bible says that Moses was "slow in speech," meaning he probably stuttered. So, if you were choosing a person to lead people out of captivity and to speak on behalf of those people to the leader of a nation, you probably wouldn't choose an old man who stuttered, right? But God did. Moses might not have been the world's first choice, but God knew he was the right man for the job.

God feels the same way about you. Even if the world doesn't believe you have what it takes to accomplish what God is calling you to do, God believes in you, and He says: "You are the right choice."

Unleash the Truth: "Remember, dear brothers and sisters, that few of you were wise in the world's eyes or powerful or wealthy when God called you." (1 Corinthians 1:26 NLT)

Digging Deeper: Do you ever feel unqualified, misunderstood, misjudged, or simply "not good enough" to do what God is calling you to do? If so, you're in good company. There are so many examples of mighty men and women of God all throughout the Bible—people the world wouldn't have chosen, but God did.

Fido 411: A male Cane Corso named Royal from Michigan has a rare universal blood type, and that allows him to donate blood to save the lives of other dogs.[3]

Weekly Tail-Waggers: Read Exodus 3 this week. Notice all of the excuses Moses gives God, trying to convince God that he isn't the right man for the job. Now, think about what God is calling you to do. What excuses are you giving God?

Michelle

Catahoula Leopard Dog

Group: Herding

Size: 20 to 26 inches; 50 to 90 pounds

Origin: When the first settlers arrived in Louisiana, they discovered beautiful, wooded land, but they also found that those woods were overrun with wild hogs. So, they came up with a solution. They bred their own herding dogs with dogs belonging to area Native Americans. The result? A tough, ferocious dog who could take on wild hogs and then some! In 1979, they were officially named Louisiana Catahoula Leopard Dog.[1]

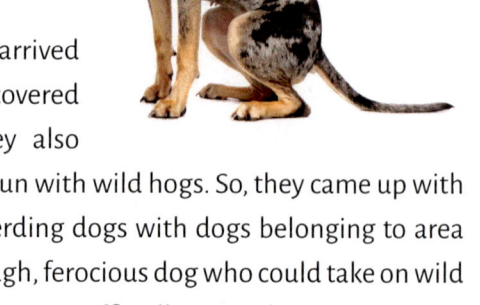

Piglet, a Catahoula Leopard Dog owned by Lori Wells, was named the 2017 ACE (Award for Canine Excellence) in the search and rescue category for Piglet's many hours of service.

AKC: The Catahoula Leopard Dog was recorded in the AKC Foundation Stock Service in 1996.

Making the Cut

The Catahoula Leopard Dog was added to the AKC Foundation Stock Service in 1996. (The AKC FSS is a list of all pure breeds that have not yet achieved full AKC recognition.) But as of 2023's Westminster Dog Show, the Catahoula Leopard Dog had not been admitted as one of the more than two hundred dog breeds allowed to compete for Best in Show at Westminster. It's quite a process for a dog breed to gain eligibility to participate in the highly regarded Westminster Dog Show, and though many folks love the Catahoula Leopard Dog breed, they are still waiting for their beloved breed to be granted that golden ticket. But does that make the Catahoula Leopard Dog any less special? Or any less important? No, it certainly does not. Because Catahoula Leopard Dogs excel at herding livestock, hunting wild game, providing protection, assisting as search and rescue dogs, and also serving as police dogs. Bottom line, they matter, whether or not they ever gain admittance into the Westminster Dog Show.

Like the Catahoula Leopard Dog, have you ever been overlooked or not chosen or denied the opportunity to participate in something that you truly desired to do? If you're like most, you probably answered yes. Life is full of disappointments and sometimes we go through rejection, and that's never fun. But I want you to know this—you matter. You are important. And God has a plan for your life. So never let negative circumstances or closed doors make you think less of yourself. Always remember that God created you, and if you've given your life to Him, He promises to direct your steps. You can trust Him with your life, and you can feel good about the person He has created you to be.

Unleash the Truth: "For we are God's masterpiece. He has created us anew in Christ Jesus, so we can do the good things he planned for us long ago." (Ephesians 2:10 NLT)

Digging Deeper: Have you ever felt overlooked? How do you deal with those feelings when you feel rejected?

Fido 411: The Catahoula Leopard Dog is the state dog of Louisiana.

Weekly Tail-Waggers: Pray this tonight before you go to sleep: "Father God, thank You for approving me and choosing me to be Your child. Help me not to dwell on rejections or closed doors. Instead, help me look to my future with excitement, knowing You have a great plan for me. Amen."

Michelle

Cavalier King Charles Spaniel

GROUP Toy

SIZE 12 to 13 inches; 13 to 18 pounds

ORIGIN This breed is a cross between spaniels and Asian toy breeds. It was named for King Charles I of England. His son, King Charles II, was so captivated by his dogs that some say he spent more time and attention on them than he did on running the country.

Although a popular choice for a companion, this dog has never won Best in Show at Westminster.

AKC 1995

Follow Closely

Cavaliers are one of the happiest, sweetest dog breeds around. If their tails aren't wagging, it's very rare. Cavaliers have never met a stranger, which makes them very good therapy dogs but pretty awful watchdogs. They crave affection, and they respond very well to praise and treats. (But don't give them too many treats because they can easily become overweight, which is bad for their overall health.)

With a Cavalier as a pet, you'll never be alone. A Cavalier is most content when it is sitting on your lap or lying next to you on the couch. This precious pooch wants to be touching you at all times, which is why it'll be your constant companion. Seriously, a Cavalier will follow you wherever you go—even into the bathroom!

We can learn a lot from the Cavalier King Charles Spaniel. If we would adore our heavenly Father as much as a Cavalier loves its master and follow as closely after God as a Cavalier follows its owner, our lives would be much happier. In fact, if we had tails, they would wag even more than a Cavalier's tail. Decide today to love your heavenly Father and to follow Him. You might be wondering how to start. Well, pray and tell God how much you love Him and read the Bible so you'll know His ways and can follow after Him.

Unleash the Truth: "But Ruth replied, 'Don't urge me to leave you or to turn back from you. Where you go I will go, and where you stay I will stay. Your people will be my people and your God my God.'" (Ruth 1:16)

Digging Deeper: Do you take time to tell God how much you love Him every day? Do you enjoy spending time with Him by reading the Bible and praying? The more you do those things, the more you'll want to—that's a promise.

Fido 411: Lots of celebrities such as Jennifer Love Hewitt, Courteney Cox, the late Frank Sinatra, Jaclyn Smith, Tom Selleck, Kristin Davis, Brad Paisley, and Sylvester Stallone (to name a few) have owned and loved Cavalier King Charles Spaniels.

Weekly Tail-Waggers: A prayer journal is a great way to spend time with your heavenly Father. If you have trouble praying, why not write out your prayers in a notebook? It can be as simple as, "I love You, God. Thank You for being my best friend."

Michelle

Chesapeake Bay Retriever

Group: Sporting

Size: 21 to 26 inches; 55 to 80 pounds

Origin: This retriever is an American breed developed to hunt ducks in bad weather and rough water conditions. They are descended from two Newfoundland pups mixed with various hounds and Irish Water Spaniels.[1]

Although "Chessies" have been competing at the Westminster Dog Show since 1877, they have never taken an award above fourth in their group.[2] However, they are strong competitors in conformation, retriever trials, hunting tests, and companion events.[3]

AKC: 1878

Study, Learn, Grow

The Chesapeake Bay Retriever is a true American classic that almost wasn't. The two pups from which the breed is developed nearly went down with a ship off the coast of Maryland in 1807. Eventually sold to different owners, their offspring went on to become the darlings of duck clubs all along Chesapeake Bay.

Chessies have a water-resistant double coat and a strong, muscular body. They are smart, can think for themselves, and are known for their amazing memory. Once they learn something, they never forget it. Even if it's a bad habit. That's why the AKC strongly recommends that Chessie owners start training their dogs as puppies. It's important to develop good habits and behaviors early.[4]

That's true for people too. No one is born with good manners or a good work ethic. Those things are taught. Baby Christians need instruction, too, because we don't usually get a divine download the minute we accept Jesus as Savior. To grow as Christians, we must spend time reading the Bible to learn how we should live. Then we have to put into practice what we learn. If we don't, we don't grow. If a human baby doesn't grow according to medical expectations, we call that failure to thrive. Christians who fail to grow are powerless and become targets for Satan's schemes. Failure to thrive as a Christian can cause unnecessary pain and suffering. To avoid it, make the study of God's Word a priority. You'll never regret it.

Unleash the Truth: "Intelligent people are always ready to learn. Their ears are open for knowledge." (Proverbs 18:15 NLT)

"I will study your commandments and reflect on your ways." (Psalm 119:15 NLT)

Digging Deeper: Think about how much time you spend each day reading the Bible or listening to biblical instruction. Do you ever give it a thought outside church? Do you have a daily Bible reading plan or time set aside for that purpose?

Fido 411: The state of Maryland loves its hunting dogs and is especially proud of their Chesapeake Bay Retriever. So much so that they named it their official state dog in 1964.

Weekly Tail-Waggers: Make it a practice to spend time reading the Bible every day. A chapter each day is a good target (except maybe for especially long chapters like Psalm 119). Ask God to help you remember what you read and understand what He wants you to know.

Wendy

Chihuahua

Group: Toy

Size: 5 to 8 inches; up to 6 pounds

Origin: Chihuahuas come from an ancient Central American breed known as Techichi, which was thought to be a part of Aztec leader Montezuma's fabled treasure that was lost to history. However, in the mid-1800s, Americans found that a number of these little dogs survived and could be found in the Mexican state of Chihuahua, which borders Texas, Arizona, and New Mexico.

Chihuahuas have never won Best in Show at Westminster. One did, however, win best in Group in 1984.

AKC: 1904

Shake It Off!

Chihuahuas are famous for being the smallest breed around with Yorkies coming in a close second. You might say that Chihuahuas are little bitty dogs with great big personalities. They are devoted and spirited.

There are two types of Chihuahuas—Apple Heads and Deer Heads. Like the names suggest, Apple Heads have round heads like apples while Deer Heads have a much narrower face that truly resembles the face of a deer. Chihuahuas also come in both smooth coat and long coat and a variety of colors.[1]

Whether an Apple Head or a Deer Head, or a smooth coat or a long coat, these little dogs all have one thing in common—they tend to get nervous around new people or when put into new environments. In fact, they can become so anxious that they actually shake uncontrollably. Chihuahua owners know that in order to comfort their shaking pets, they need to speak quietly and calmly, and if at all possible, remove the pet from the situation causing the anxiety.

Have you ever been so scared that you started shaking? Maybe you didn't shake on the outside but you were shaking like crazy on the inside. Fear can do that to you. You might get really nervous when you have to meet new people. Or, maybe you get really anxious when you have a big test coming up. When we feel anxious or scared, we can go to our heavenly Father and let His words comfort us. We can meditate on scriptures such as: "The LORD is a mighty tower where his people can run for safety" (Proverbs 18:10 CEV), and "I asked the LORD for help, and he saved me from all my fears" (Psalm 34:4 CEV). When you think about those promises instead of focusing on your fears, you'll feel like you're wrapped in a blanket of calm and the shaking will stop.

Just like the Chihuahua runs to its owner for comfort, you can run to your God for comfort. He's got you!

Unleash the Truth: "Cast all your anxiety on him because he cares for you." (1 Peter 5:7)

Digging Deeper: What scares you the most? Do you struggle every single day with fear? If so, cast your cares on God but also tell someone you trust about what you're going through.

Fido 411: Did you know that the most famous "purse puppy" to ever be toted around by a celebrity was Tinker Bell, which belonged to Paris Hilton? Tink lived to be fourteen years old.

Weekly Tail-Waggers: Grab your journal and write the letters F E A R vertically, and now write this beside each letter: False Evidence Appearing Real. Many times, that's what fear is—false evidence appearing real—but we get so worked up about what might happen that we actually shake. Well, don't shake in fear today, shake it off instead. God has got you!

Michelle

Chinese Crested

Toy

11 to 13 inches; 8 to 12 pounds

The exact beginnings of this breed are not really known but the hairless variety has been in China since the sixteenth century. This breed became popular with Chinese sailors because the Chinese Crested dogs would kill all of the rats on board, helping to keep the ship disease-free. Some say the breed arrived in the United States in the late 1800s; others disagree. But one thing that is for sure is that the American Chinese Crested Club formed in the United States in 1979.[1]

Though this breed is adored by many families, it has never won Best in Show at Westminster. It has, however, won several "Ugliest Dog" contests.

1991

God Has a Way of Escape—You Can Trust Him!

The Chinese Crested comes in two very different-looking varieties—the Powderpuff and the Hairless. As you might have guessed, the Powderpuffs are covered with a long silky coat while the hairless version is not. The Hairless is not actually *completely* hairless. It grows hair on its head, tail, and feet. Interestingly, the Powderpuff and Hairless versions can be born in the same litter!

Though this breed is happiest at its owner's side, lounging around and loving life, it is actually quite crafty! Some call this dog a "Houdini Hound" (referring to the famous magician/escape artist Harry Houdini) because a Chinese Crested dog can literally escape any backyard! They are little dogs, but they can easily jump four feet in the air from a standing position! And, they can climb too! Plus, they have no fear of scaling a fence, tree, or whatever will provide a means of escape. Experts advise owners of this breed to put up a six-foot fence to keep their beloved pets safe inside.[2]

Speaking of escaping—have you ever wanted to escape a bad situation? Maybe you are friends with a group of kids who sometimes treat people badly. You find yourself feeling uncomfortable when they start making fun of others, but you're not sure what to do. You want to leave—but how? You wonder if they'll make fun of you once you leave the group. You convince yourself it might be easier to stay and listen, but your heart tells you it's time to move on. Don't worry! God will give you the courage to walk away. The Bible tells us that God will provide a way of escape every time, meaning that He will help you do the hard things. You're not alone. You can trust Him. So, go ahead! Walk away faster than a Chinese Crested can scale a fence. God will go with you.

Unleash the Truth: "You are tempted in the same way that everyone else is tempted. But God can be trusted not to let you be tempted too much, and he will show you how to escape from your temptations." (1 Corinthians 10:13 CEV)

Digging Deeper: Have you ever felt trapped, like there is no way of escaping a bad situation? If so, you should tell a trusted adult about what you're going through, but also, turn to God! He always provides a way of escape.

Fido 411: These dogs are often called "the Dr. Seuss Dog" because they look like characters from Dr. Seuss books.

Weekly Tail-Waggers: This week, why not sit next to the kid at school who sits alone every day? You just might be that person's way of escaping loneliness.

Michelle

Chinese Shar-Pei
(Shar-PAY)

GROUP Non-Sporting

SIZE 18 to 20 inches; 40 to 60 pounds

ORIGIN The Chinese Shar-Pei originated in the Kwantung province of Southern China during the Han Dynasty (200 BC).[1]

The Shar-Pei took home Best in Group honors at Westminster in 2011 and has placed in the Non-Sporting group seven other times.[2] The Shar-Pei also does well in obedience, rally, agility, herding, flyball, lure coursing, and freestyle dance competitions.[3]

AKC 1992

The Outside Doesn't Always Match the Inside

The Shar-Pei is an ancient breed. It was originally an all-purpose farm dog and was later used in the fighting ring. In theory, their wrinkled skin made it harder for another dog to get a good hold on them. Fortunately, Shar-Pei were really no match for larger, stronger breeds, and soon disappeared from the grisly sport. The name Shar-Pei means "rough, sandy coat" or "sandpaper coat."

The Shar-Pei's wrinkled face and hippopotamus-shaped muzzle gives it a stern look. But looks can be deceiving. Behind that stern (or sad, depending on how you view it) expression and sandpaper fur beats the heart of a true companion dog. Shar-Pei are good natured, loyal, intelligent, and clean. When properly trained and socialized, they make wonderful family dogs.[4]

Like a Shar-Pei, it's kind of hard to tell anything about a person by looking at the outside. Only a person's heart can reveal what they are really like. It may not be obvious at first, but people's true character will eventually show in how they live their lives.

Sometimes people can fool us into thinking they are something they are not. But they can never fool God. No matter what we seem on the outside, God always knows who we really are. He knows our thoughts. He knows our hearts. The Bible says He searches us to reward us based on our conduct.

At the same time, it's really important that we don't judge people based on the things we see. The way a person is dressed or the things they do may or may not be what they're really like. Only God can see what's going on in their head and heart. We can easily make a mistake, but God never will. His judgment is the only one that counts because it's the only one that is 100 percent accurate.

The Shar-Pei's lesson to us is never mind someone else's heart. It's God's job to judge them. Pay attention to your own heart. Make sure to keep it pure before Him.

Unleash the Truth: "As water reflects the face, so one's life reflects the heart." (Proverbs 27:19)

"I the Lord search the heart and examine the mind, to reward each person according to their conduct, according to what their deeds deserve." (Jeremiah 17:10)

"The Lord does not look at the things people look at. People look at the outward appearance, but the Lord looks at the heart." (1 Samuel 16:7)

Digging Deeper: Have you ever been guilty of judging someone based on their appearance?

Fido 411: The Shar-Pei has a blue-black tongue. The only other dog with this characteristic is the Chow Chow, but the two breeds are not related.[5]

Weekly Tail-Waggers: This week ask God to examine your heart. Pray Psalm 139:23–24 and ask God to lead you in the right way.

Wendy

Chow Chow

GROUP Non-Sporting

SIZE 17 to 20 inches; 45 to 70 pounds

ORIGIN The Chow is one of the oldest breeds in the world. They were often owned by Chinese nobles. They are portrayed in ancient Chinese artifacts as early as the Han dynasty in 206 BC but are believed to be much older. They were first presented in America in the 1890s.

The Chow has not taken top awards at dog shows but several famous people have owned this breed including artist Georgia O'Keeffe, President Calvin Coolidge, Martha Stewart, and Elvis Presley.[1]

AKC 1903

Love Adapts

The Chow Chow is an intelligent, independent, and often very standoffish dog. In fact, if not properly socialized as pups, Chows can be quite territorial and unfriendly, usually only bonding with one person in the household. To have a good experience with a Chow, it's recommended to have some sort of consistent obedience training early in the dog's life. This breed is not right for every home, but with proper socializing and training, it can become a great family pet. And, it makes a great watchdog!

Chows don't always "play nicely" with others, especially other animals. Because of their hunting instincts, they've been known to go after smaller dogs and cats. However, if you introduce a Chow puppy into the family, and it grows up around other animals, there's a chance everyone will get along just fine. Still, some experts suggest that Chows behave better when they are the only pet.

How about you? Are you easy to get along with, or are you a little more difficult, kind of like the Chow Chow? Do you play well with others? You know, the Bible talks a lot about getting along with one another. First Corinthians 13:5 says, "Love does not insist on its own rights or its own way, for it is not self-seeking" (AMPC). In other words, love adapts. If you're walking in love, you'll be pleasant to be around. And, when you don't get your way because someone else in the family gets his or her way, you'll be OK with it. Be honest with yourself: Can you still be happy if you don't get your way all the time? Or do you pout and act awful, demanding your way?

If you're a little bit like the temperamental Chow Chow, ask God to help you become more like Him. God will fill you up with His love, and that will cause you to become more agreeable.

Unleash the Truth: "Do all that you can to live in peace with everyone." (Romans 12:18 NLT)

Digging Deeper: Have you ever been around someone who is really hard to get along with? How did that make you feel? What can you do to live at peace with everyone?

Fido 411: Did you know that as a Chow ages, its tongue turns from pink to a blue/black color? The only other dog with this unique-colored tongue is the Shar-Pei. [2]

Weekly Tail-Waggers: Here's your assignment: try memorizing 1 Corinthians 13:4–13. Maybe do one verse a day. You can do it!

Michelle

Cocker Spaniel

GROUP Sporting

SIZE 13.5 to 15.5 inches; 20 to 30 pounds

ORIGIN The Cocker Spaniel is thought to have begun in Spain because of the name. The dogs were used as hunters. For years European and English Spaniels were known as either land Spaniels or water Spaniels. By the nineteenth century, breed standards for dog shows were in the works for a few specific breeds. One of the breeds was the Cocker, so named because it mostly hunted a type of bird know as a woodcock. This eventually led to the modern Cocker Spaniel.

The Cocker Spaniel has won Best in Show four times at Westminster with back-to-back wins in 1940 and 1941. It also took the American Kennel Club championship in 2017.

AKC The Cocker Spaniel is one of the first nine breeds registered by the AKC in 1878.

Little Dog, Big Accomplishments

The Cocker Spaniel is the smallest member of the Sporting group. But don't underestimate a Cocker Spaniel because of its smallish body and curly ears! This little dog has won the Westminster Dog Show four times, while many, many other dog breeds in its group have never even placed!

In a lot of ways, we can be like these small but mighty pups with God's help!

You may have heard stories about a guy named David in the Bible. He was the smallest of his seven brothers, and nobody really expected him to do much with his life besides being a shepherd. But God had bigger plans for David. David was the only Israelite brave enough to fight the giant, Goliath—and he won! He went on to become one of Israel's greatest kings. Even though David looked little, God called him to do big things.

God calls us to do big things too. He has a special plan for your life that is bigger than you can even imagine! No matter how small you may feel, remember that God created you just the way you are with a specific purpose in mind. And He will help you accomplish that purpose. Listen to the messages He is sending you and seek after Him and His ways. Follow where He is guiding you. Just like a Cocker Spaniel, you can be little in stature, but big in heart! You're not too young or too little to make a big impact for the kingdom of God.

Unleash the Truth: "I can do all this through him who gives me strength." (Philippians 4:13)

Digging Deeper: What big things do you feel God is calling you to do?

Fido 411: Did you know the main character, Lady, in the Disney movie *Lady and the Tramp* (1955) is a golden Cocker Spaniel?[1]

Weekly Tail-Waggers: In your journal, keep a list of your dreams and ideas. Start praying over them and asking God if they are a part of His big plan for your life.

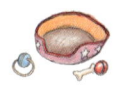

Michelle

Collie

GROUP Herding

SIZE 22 to 26 inches; 50 to 75 pounds

ORIGIN The Collie was originally bred as a herding dog in Scotland and Northern England. It became a favorite of Queen Victoria in the 1860s and, as a result, became very popular. The breed includes both Rough and Smooth coat varieties.[1]

Collies have competed at Westminster since 1877. Smooth and Rough Collies are judged separately and were part of the working group until 1983 when herding dogs became a separate group. Both varieties have made a respectable showing at Westminster, but only the Rough Collie has ever taken Best in Show. It has also won Best in Group six times.[2]

AKC 1885

Love Deeply

Collies are beautiful dogs with seriously intelligent faces. Maybe that's because they really are smart. Immortalized in books and the American TV series Lassie during the 1950s, they have become one of the best-loved dogs of all time.

Not only are they beautiful and skillful herding dogs, Collies have a real affection for people. It's one of their most endearing qualities. In the TV series Lassie, Timmy was always being rescued by his Collie. The way Lassie lovingly watched over Timmy was a true testament to the Collie's character.

Jesus didn't have a Collie to point to as an example, but if He had, He might have told His disciples to love like a Collie. A Collie's love is unconditional. They are loyal and protective, patient and kind. They show their love for people just the way the Bible describes in 1 Corinthians 13:4–7. In a world that is often hateful and spiteful, love is, and should be, a believer's most obvious character trait. After all, love is the greatest.

Unleash the Truth: "Above all, love each other deeply, because love covers over a multitude of sins." (1 Peter 4:8)

Digging Deeper: What does it mean to love others? Does it mean you have to feel all warm and fuzzy about a person? Read 1 Corinthians 13. Take special note of verses 4–7.

Fido 411: Traditionally, Rough Collies helped manage sheep in their home pastures and served as their guards. Smooth Collies worked with drovers to get sheep to market, which required a slightly different set of skills.[3]

Weekly Tail-Waggers: Keep in mind that love is not necessarily a feeling. Being kind and patient with others is a choice. You can choose to love others, even when they aren't very loving toward you. Make up your mind to love others, no matter what.

Wendy

Czechoslovakian Vlcak

(VIL-chalk)

GROUP Working

SIZE 23.5 to 25.5 inches tall; 44 to 57 pounds

ORIGIN Originally, the Czechoslovakian Vlcak (also known as the Czechoslovakian Wolfdog) was bred to work border control in Czechoslovakia in the 1950s. Today, they are used as search-and-rescue dogs, as well as for tracking and herding.[1]

The Czechoslovakian Vlcak has never won at Westminster.

AKC The Czechoslovakian Vlcak was recorded in the AKC Foundation Stock Service (FSS) in 2001, and it's been able to compete in AKC Companion Events since 2010. The first American litter of Czechoslovakian Vlcaks was bred in the United States in 2009.

Run Your Race with Endurance!

Czechoslovakian Vlcaks, or CSVs for short, are generally muscular, lean, and weatherproof. These magnificent dogs really look rather wolflike and can be either yellow gray, silver gray, or dark gray. And, their eyes are yellow to amber in color. With their thick coats, CSVs are made for the great outdoors, and they love it—especially water and snow.

Because of their purpose—being search-and-rescue dogs—CSVs are put through endurance tests before they are assigned to such important duties. In fact, the CSVs must run alongside a bicycle for 60 miles, and that distance must be completed in 8 hours![2]

Have you ever had to complete an endurance test in PE class, or maybe you had to go through such a test to earn a badge in a scouting program? They can be challenging for sure! But some endurance tests aren't physically challenging, they are spiritually challenging. That's why the Apostle Paul wrote in Hebrews that we are to run with perseverance the race marked out for us (Hebrews 12:1). Do you know another word for perseverance? Endurance! Paul wrote this so that we wouldn't give up as we run our individual races. You see, life is a race. We don't want to quit moving toward that finish line simply because we grow tired or because circumstances become too hard. No, we want to press forward, fulfilling all that God has for us to do along the way, right? Then when we get there, we will hear God say, "Well done, my good and faithful child." So, run that race. Like the Czechoslovakian Vlcaks, let's run with endurance—never stopping, never giving up! You can do it because God has given you everything you need to finish strong.

Unleash the Truth: "Therefore, since we are surrounded by such a great cloud of witnesses, let us throw off everything that hinders and the sin that so easily entangles. And let us run with perseverance the race marked out for us." (Hebrews 12:1)

Digging Deeper: Have you ever thought of your life as a race? Maybe you're not a very fast or skilled runner in the natural, but spiritually speaking, you are a champion athlete! Now go forth and run your race, fulfilling your purpose here on earth.

Fido 411: Did you know that the Vlcak is a result of a biological experiment crossing a German Shepherd and a Carpathian wolf?

Weekly Tail-Waggers: Grab your journal and write down the things you feel God is calling you to do in life. If you don't know, ask Him to begin to reveal His plans for you. Next, read the verse Jeremiah 29:11. That way, you'll have no doubt that God has a wonderful, very specific plan for your life.

Michelle

Dachshund

(DAHK-sund)

Group Hound

Size *standard*—8 to 9 inches; 16 to 32 pounds, *miniature*—5 to 6 inches; 11 pounds and under

Origin The dachshund was bred in Germany in the 1500s.

Even though the dachshund is almost always in the top ten most popular dogs in the US, it has never won Best in Show at Westminster. It has, however, won Best of Group ten times![1]

AKC 1885

Be Bold!

Dachshunds are my very favorite breed. (We have two long-haired miniature doxies in our family now!) They are very special little dogs, and they are fierce hunters. In fact, in German, the word *dachshund* means "badger hound" because these long, low-to-the-ground dogs successfully hunt badgers. Brilliant diggers, dachshunds dig into the badgers' burrows and attack, which makes them invaluable to German farmers. You see, badgers were a real problem for the farmers because they ate all of the farmers' crops!

Though dachshunds originally came from Germany, it was England that first turned Doxies from hunters into beloved pets, and it wasn't until the 1870s that this special breed made its way to the United States.[2]

Often called wiener dogs, weenie dogs, sausage dogs, or hot dogs, this adorable breed has several varieties: short-haired, long-haired, and wire-haired, and thirteen different color combinations! Doxies come in different patterns too, such as: dapple, double dapple, brindle, piebald, brindle piebald, and sable.

But no matter what you call them or what they look like, there's one thing all dachshunds have in common—they are bold! They are known for their determined, spirited nature, and their ability to push fear aside and hunt badgers or take on a much larger dog. Kind of like David in the Bible. Remember him? He was a shepherd boy—the smallest in his family—who killed a lion and a bear to protect his father's sheep. So, when the giant, Goliath, came against their people and no one could defeat him, David volunteered and took him down with a sling (sort of like an ancient slingshot) and a couple of stones. Everyone else looked at Goliath and said, "He's too big to kill," but David looked at Goliath and with boldness said, "He's too big to miss!"

That's the kind of attitude we need to have when we face giants in our lives. Maybe you're facing the invisible giant of fear—fear you won't be accepted by others, or fear that you won't have any close friends. Whatever giant you're battling today, you don't have to battle alone. You can have that same boldness that David had—the same boldness that dachshunds have—and you can face any giant head-on, knowing God is with you and in you! Be bold in your faith and watch those giants fall.

Unleash the Truth: "The Lord is my light and my salvation—so why should I be afraid? The Lord is my fortress, protecting me from danger, so why should I tremble?" (Psalm 27:1 NLT)

Digging Deeper: Have you ever stood up to a bully or faced an invisible giant in your life? If you answered yes, what gave you the boldness to stand strong?

Fido 411: Did you know that a 2008 study in the journal of *Applied Animal Behaviour Science* named the dachshund as the most aggressive of all dog breeds?[3]

Weekly Tail-Waggers: Grab your journal and write down the giants in your life today. Now, draw a big X over them and thank God that He is with you as you boldly face your giants. Don't be afraid to ask a parent or a trusted friend to pray with you about these giants.

Michelle

Dalmatian

GROUP — Non-Sporting

SIZE — 19 to 24 inches; 45 to 70 pounds

ORIGIN — The true origin of the Dalmatian is not known, but spotted dogs are shown as companions to people even in cave drawings. Their name comes from the region of Dalmatia in modern-day Croatia, which is believed to be their birthplace.[1]

Although Dalmatians have never won a Best in Show at Westminster, they have placed in their group an impressive thirty-five times. They compete successfully in many types of competitions, including one for Dalmatians only—Road Dog.[2]

AKC — 1888

In It for the Long Run

Dalmatians get along well with horses. During the 1800s, Dalmatians in England became popular as "carriage dogs." They were often kept to run alongside the carriages to keep the horses calm and keep an eye out for danger. They never seemed to tire out. Later, in the US, Dalmatians were used as "fire-house dogs" to run with horse-drawn fire engines. Their barking helped clear the way ahead of the fire engine.[3]

Running for such long distances requires strength and stamina—for dogs *and* people. And whether the race is a literal run or the marathon we call life, we need strength and stamina to get through it. If we're going to run with the big dogs, we have to take care of our bodies. But our health only goes so far. No matter how healthy a person is, sometimes that's just not enough. But here's the good news. Believers have a secret source of strength a lot of people don't know about. Isn't that cool?

The Bible tells us that those who put their hope in the Lord will renew their strength. When we're tired—when we've reached the end of our own ability—God says if we put our hope in Him, He'll give us strength to soar on wings like eagles. He'll help us run and not grow weary. And he'll help us walk and never faint. Knowing God and trusting Him in all of the things we face in life is the secret weapon we need to run our race—and win!

Unleash the Truth: "But those who hope in the Lord will renew their strength. They will soar on wings like eagles; they will run and not grow weary, they will walk and not be faint." (Isaiah 40:31)

Digging Deeper: Have you ever felt overwhelmed with all the things you *have* to do and things you know you *should* do?

Fido 411: About 30 percent of Dalmatians have hearing loss in one or both ears. This is due to the lack of melanin-producing cells in their inner ear. Those cells are also what give the Dalmatian its spotted coat. The reason these cells affect the dog's hearing is not yet understood.[4]

Weekly Tail-Waggers: An acrostic poem is one that uses each letter of a word or phrase to build a poem. It can be separate words, or it can be phrases that connect to make a sentence. For example, if we were to create an acrostic poem using *dog*, it might look like

Duty	*or*	**D**etermined to
Observation		**O**bey me, so I
Good boy		**G**ive him treats.

Create an acrostic poem using the letters from the word *hope*. Write a word that tells how God helps those who put their hope in Him, or tell something about the character of God. For example: *H* could be "helps" or "holy."

Wendy

Doberman Pinscher

Group Working

Size 24 to 28 inches; 60 to 100 pounds

Origin In the 1800s, a tax collector in Germany named Louis Dobermann worked to breed a strong, dependable dog to defend him as he collected taxes. The dogs he bred were the first of the Doberman Pinschers we have today.

The Doberman has won Westminster Best in Show four times—1939, 1952, 1953, and 1989.

AKC 1908

The Alpha Dog

The Doberman Pinscher is loyal and fearless. With their sharp minds and muscular bodies, they make great guard dogs. Although they are friendly with their owners, this breed isn't one you want to approach before asking the owners if it's OK.

Doberman Pinschers not only look like leaders of the canine world, they actually possess strong leadership qualities. In fact, if a human in the home doesn't step up and act as the leader, the Doberman will try to assume the alpha dog role of the family! (An alpha dog in a group is confident and strong-willed, so it naturally leads the others.) But if a Doberman assumes the alpha dog role in a family of humans, that dog will not follow the humans' commands and may expect the humans to follow its lead. This, of course, can be a problem and cause disorder within a household because there can only be one leader.

We all need a leader. As Christians, God is our leader. The Bible even describes God as our Alpha and Omega! He has made rules for us that keep us safe and give us the best life we can have. When we follow Him, we can know we're making good choices that will lead us into the best life. Look to God as your Alpha, and He will take care of you!

Unleash the Truth: "Without wise leadership, a nation falls; there is safety in having many advisers." (Proverbs 11:14 NLT)

Digging Deeper: Do you trust God as your leader? What is one thing you feel He has been telling you to do this week?

Fido 411: No one is really sure what the term *pinscher* means! The best guess is that it came from the German word for "terrier," even though a Doberman isn't a terrier.[1]

Weekly Tail-Waggers: In your journal, make a list of words that describe a good leader. Do those words describe God? Do they describe you? Do they describe anyone else you know?

Michelle

French Bulldog

GROUP Non-Sporting

SIZE 11 to 13 inches; under 28 pounds

ORIGIN French Bulldogs are descended from toy Bulldogs bred in England in the 1800s. When English owners of these small lapdogs moved to France, the breed quickly became popular with the French.[1]

French Bulldogs have never been awarded Best in Show at Westminster, but a Frenchie did win the Best in Group in 2010. They have placed in their group an additional twenty-two times. In general, Frenchies do well in conformation (how well they measure up to the breed standard) and companion events.[2]

AKC 1898

Close to You

Frenchies were meant to be lap dogs. And they love it. Their favorite activity is snuggling. They're famous for having no boundaries when it comes to their favorite person. Wherever that person is—a Frenchie wants to be too. They like to stay close to and keep a watchful eye on their owner's activities. They are true companion dogs.[3]

That adoring attitude is what Frenchie owners love about them. And it makes them want to spoil their precious pooches even more.

Like a Frenchie who never takes its eyes off its owner, God would like to see that same thing in us. He wants us to stay close to Him. He knows that the more time we spend with Him and the more we keep our eyes focused on Him, the deeper our relationship with Him will be. He wants that. He wants it for Him. And He wants it for us.

Here's a news bulletin for you: God loves you. And He *wants* to spend time with you. He *wants* you to take the time to sit in His lap for a while and cuddle up close. He *wants* you to cling to Him so you'll have a better relationship with Him. And you know what else? The more you know Him and the better your relationship with Him—the better prepared you will be for whatever life throws at you. And just like Frenchie owners like to spoil their adoring pups, God will spoil you too by pouring blessing and favor over you because you make it a point to stay close to Him.

Unleash the Truth: "Serve only the Lord your God and fear him alone. Obey his commands, listen to his voice, and cling to him." (Deuteronomy 13:4 NLT)

"Come close to God, and God will come close to you." (James 4:8 NLT)

Digging Deeper: How much time do you spend on a regular basis reading your Bible? Do you pray and think about what you read?

Fido 411: Many airlines will not allow French Bulldogs to be transported on their aircraft. The Frenchie's short snout can cause breathing problems. In addition, the stress of flying and sometimes uncomfortably warm temperatures can be life-threatening.[4]

Weekly Tail-Waggers: Make it a habit to spend time with God every day. Use a Bible app to help you with your daily reading. It will help you stay on track.

Wendy

German Shepherd

Group Herding

Size 22 to 26 inches; 50 to 90 pounds

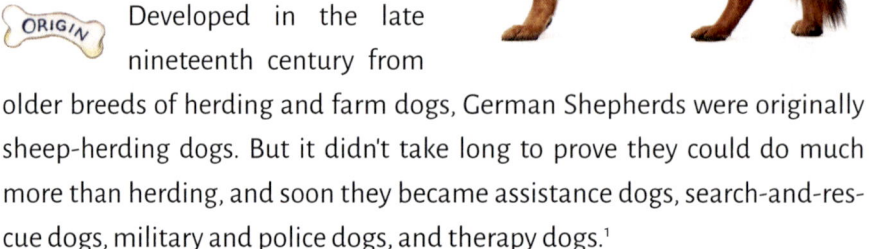

Origin Developed in the late nineteenth century from older breeds of herding and farm dogs, German Shepherds were originally sheep-herding dogs. But it didn't take long to prove they could do much more than herding, and soon they became assistance dogs, search-and-rescue dogs, military and police dogs, and therapy dogs.[1]

A German Shepherd has won Best in Show at Westminster twice—once in 1987 with Manhattan (nicknamed "Hatter") and again in 2017 with Rumor Has It.[2]

AKC 1908

Loyal to the End

Constant companion. Loyal to the end. Those are two descriptions you'll often hear from families who own German Shepherds. That loyalty runs deep within this breed and dates back to its beginnings. In fact, the Germans used these dogs as Casualty dogs, or Mercy dogs, in World War I to find wounded soldiers on the battlefield and take them medical supplies. Sometimes, however, a Mercy dog would find a soldier who couldn't be saved and would stay with him until he died. Loyal to the very end.

You know who else is a constant companion and loyal to the end? Jesus. The Bible tells us He is a friend who sticks closer than a brother (Proverbs 18:24). He promises that He will never leave us or forsake us, meaning He will stay with us until the very end. Isn't that good news? No matter how lonely you may feel at times, you have a loyal friend in Jesus. Like those Mercy dogs, Jesus knows just what you need, and He will bring it into your life at just the right time. You can trust Him.

Unleash the Truth: "This is how we know what love is: Jesus Christ laid down his life for us." (1 John 3:16)

Digging Deeper: Have you ever felt lonely? Did you know that even though you can't see Jesus, He is always with you? It's true!

Fido 411: Ever heard of Rin Tin Tin? This famous German Shepherd, rescued from a World War I battlefield by an American soldier named Duncan Lee, became a movie star! Lee trained the brilliant pooch to work in silent films.[3]

Weekly Tail-Waggers: Loyal means "having or showing complete and constant support for someone or something" according to the Learner's Dictionary.[4] Do you have a best friend who is loyal? Why don't you thank that person for being loyal to you and always having your back? And, while you're at it, why not take a minute to thank Jesus for being your loyal friend too?

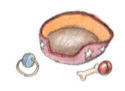

Michelle

German Shorthaired Pointer

Sporting

21 to 25 inches; 45 to 70 pounds

The German Shorthaired Pointer originated in the 1800s as German hunters were seeking the perfect bird dog. They wanted an all-purpose hunting dog, and that's what they achieved because this pointer became a good retriever on land and in water. Its webbed feet have made it one of the greatest doggie swimmers ever.

The German Shorthaired Pointer has won three Best in Shows at Westminster.

1930

Special Talents

With its endurance, agility, and enthusiasm, the German Shorthaired Pointer is an all-around great hunting dog. It's a friendly breed that loves to spend time with family, especially if that time involves running around and being active. But it has one special feature that makes it stand out from all other hunting dogs: webbed feet. A German Shorthaired Pointer's webbed feet equals great swimming capabilities, so it's the perfect dog to retrieve ducks.

And guess what. God made us with special talents too.

You are good at a lot of things. Everybody is! But there are probably a few things that you are really, really good at, right? God has given all of His children unique and special gifts: talents they can use to help the church and everyone around them. That means YOU have special talents that God has given you! As Christians, it's our job to use these talents not just for our own benefit but for the benefit of everyone we encounter.

Maybe you are really good at helping your friends understand their math homework. Or maybe you're great at creating really special cards to brighten someone's day. Or maybe you're gifted with a beautiful singing voice. Whatever it is, you can be like the German Shorthaired Pointer and use your talents to help the people you love and serve the Master you adore. Now, go be a blessing!

Unleash the Truth: "We have different gifts, according to the grace given to each of us. If your gift is prophesying, then prophesy in accordance with your faith; if it is serving, then serve; if it is teaching, then teach; if it is to encourage, then give encouragement; if it is giving, then give generously; if it is to lead, do it diligently; if it is to show mercy, do it cheerfully." (Romans 12:6–8)

Digging Deeper: What spiritual gifts do you think God has given you? What special talents do you have?

Fido 411: The German Shorthaired Pointer's most predominant ancestor seems to be the German Bird Dog.1

Weekly Tail-Waggers: Ask three friends or family members to tell you something they think you are really good at. Next, return the favor by telling them a few things you think they are really good at too!

Michelle

Golden Retriever

Group Sporting

Size 21.5 to 24 inches; 55 to 75 pounds

Origin Goldens were originally bred in Scotland during the 1800s as hunting dogs who specialized in retrieving game.[1]

Goldens are one of the top three breeds in the United States, but they have never taken home a Best in Show award from Westminster. In the 2020 show, a Golden named Daniel came awfully close. He took top honors in his breed and sporting group. Although he didn't win the top award, the crowd clearly thought he should have. They chanted his name in the final round as though he was a popular sports figure.[2]

AKC 1925

Faithful Guide

Goldens were originally bred as hunting dogs. These days they're more likely to be seen in field trials and obedience competitions. They're also great at search and rescue and sniffing out explosives or drugs. But where they really shine is as guide dogs for the blind or helpers for people with disabilities.[3]

Goldens have a personality to match their sunny golden color. They are smart and easy to train. And their gentle, friendly nature makes them a perfect companion and guide. Many people depend on Goldens to guide them safely through the obstacles of life on a daily basis. This is one dog that never disappoints.[4]

There's someone else who never disappoints either. Our heavenly Father is always ready and willing to guide us in our daily lives. In the Old Testament, He guided the children of Israel through the desert with a cloud during the day and a pillar of fire at night. Today, God guides us through his Word. Everything we need to know about how to live our lives is in the Bible. Whenever you have questions about what to do or how to handle a situation, all you have to remember is: It's in the book!

Unleash the Truth: "The Lord went ahead of them. He guided them during the day with a pillar of cloud, and he provided light at night with a pillar of fire. This allowed them to travel by day or by night." (Exodus 13:21 NLT)

"Your word is a lamp to guide my feet and a light for my path." (Psalm 119:105 NLT)

Digging Deeper: Are you looking to God as your guide? Or do you look to your friends to show you what to do?

Fido 411: A Golden in Canandaigua, New York, is the new (unofficial) world record holder for the number of tennis balls one very good boy can hold in his mouth at once. Finley can hold (drum roll, please) . . . SIX tennis balls at one time! The old record of five was held by a Golden in Texas.[5]

Weekly Tail-Waggers: Do yourself a favor. Read your Bible on a regular basis. It might be a few verses or a whole chapter but try to read it every day. Think about what you read. Most important, ask God to guide you through His Word.

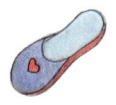

Wendy

Goldendoodle

GROUP   Crossbreed

SIZE   20 to 24 inches; 50 to 90 pounds[1]

ORIGIN   Goldendoodles are a cross between a Golden Retriever and a Poodle. They were first bred in the United States and Australia in the 1990s.[2]

Goldendoodles do not participate in conformation (how well they measure up to the breed standard) events but do well in obedience and companion contests.

AKC   Goldendoodles are not recognized by the American Kennel Club.

No Greater Love

Goldendoodles have all the personality of a Golden Retriever and all the smarts of a Poodle. So even though they aren't purebreds, they are highly sought after as guide dogs, assistance dogs, therapy dogs, and search-and-rescue workers. They make great family pets too. And like other popular breeds, they can be expensive.[3]

In 2012, singer-songwriter Usher shelled out $12,000 for a Goldendoodle puppy at a charity event. That's a lot of money to spend, especially for a crossbreed. But, obviously, Usher valued the puppy and wanted it as a gift for his two sons.[4]

You have value too. The Bible says that sin is punishable by death. That's a problem because we have *all* sinned. But God thought we were *worth* saving, so He sent His son to die in our place. God valued us and loved us so much that He was willing to give His only son to take our punishment.

Paws-itive Inspirations

Jesus left His home in heaven and came to earth so that He could give His life to save ours. He chose to obey God and become the payment for our sin. The best part is that Jesus did this willingly because He loved us so much. God didn't force him to do it. He *chose* to do it. In doing this, Jesus showed how very much He loves us. There is no greater love than that!

Unleash the Truth: "For God so loved the world that he gave his one and only Son, that whoever believes in him shall not perish but have eternal life." (John 3:16)

"But God demonstrates his own love for us in this: While we were still sinners, Christ died for us." (Romans 5:8)

"I lay down my life for the sheep. . . . No one takes it from me, but I lay it down of my own accord." (John 10:15, 18)

"Greater love has no one than this: to lay down one's life for one's friends." (John 15:13)

Digging Deeper: How do we know what sin is?

Fido 411: Goldendoodles are called Groodles in Australia. Many people love them because they are usually a good dog for people who have allergies.[5]

Weekly Tail-Waggers: Think about the price that Jesus paid for your sins. Take time today to thank Him for giving His life so that you could be saved.

Wendy

89

Great Dane

Group Working

Size 28 to 32 inches; 110 to 175 pounds

Origin The Great Dane is a very old breed that originated in Germany. In spite of their name, Great Danes have nothing to do with Denmark. The Germans used them for hunting bears and wild boar.[1]

The Great Dane has taken Best in Group five times at Westminster and placed in the group an additional seventeen times.[2] Great Danes also successfully compete in agility, tracking, obedience, flyball, and weight pulls.[3]

AKC 1887

Be Anxious for Nothing

Great Danes are one of the largest dog breeds. Once they reach adulthood, they're known for being gentle giants. They're also very social dogs who love their people. They don't do well when left alone and can develop anxiety. Anxiety sometimes leads to a condition called "bloat" which can cause death in less than an hour. Danes can actually fret and worry themselves to death.[4]

People worry too. They worry about all sorts of things. And most of the things they worry about never happen anyway! But worrying (being anxious) about what *might* happen can lead to all kinds of health problems in people just as it does in Great Danes.

The Bible tells us that worry is a sign that our faith is weak. Jesus taught us not to worry because our heavenly Father knows what we need before we even

Paws-itive Inspirations

ask. We must always remember that God is more than able to take care of us. Our job is to make our needs and requests known to Him and trust Him to take care of it. And because He is a faithful, loving God, He always does.

Unleash the Truth: "Do not be anxious about anything, but in every situation, by prayer and petition, with thanksgiving, present your requests to God." (Philippians 4:6)

"Cast all your anxiety on him because he cares for you." (1 Peter 5:7)

Digging Deeper: What kinds of things do you worry about?

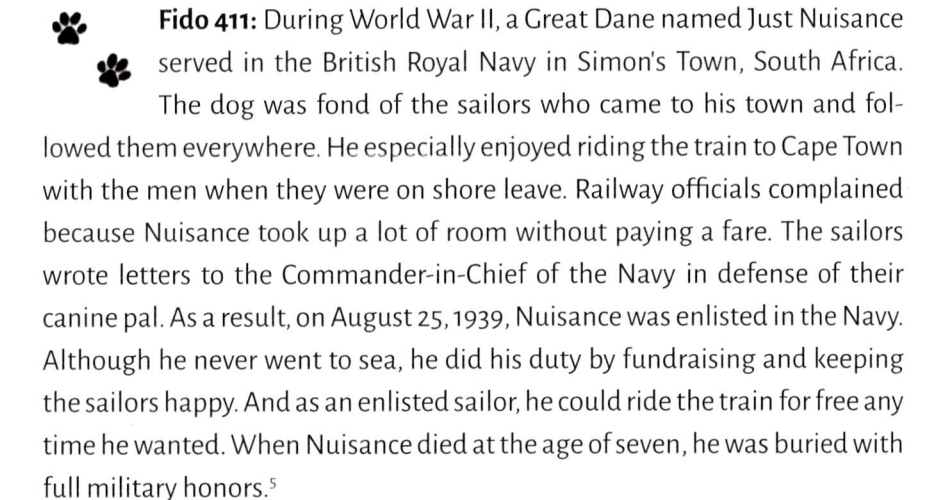

Fido 411: During World War II, a Great Dane named Just Nuisance served in the British Royal Navy in Simon's Town, South Africa. The dog was fond of the sailors who came to his town and followed them everywhere. He especially enjoyed riding the train to Cape Town with the men when they were on shore leave. Railway officials complained because Nuisance took up a lot of room without paying a fare. The sailors wrote letters to the Commander-in-Chief of the Navy in defense of their canine pal. As a result, on August 25, 1939, Nuisance was enlisted in the Navy. Although he never went to sea, he did his duty by fundraising and keeping the sailors happy. And as an enlisted sailor, he could ride the train for free any time he wanted. When Nuisance died at the age of seven, he was buried with full military honors.[5]

Weekly Tail-Waggers: Make a list of the things that you tend to worry about. Maybe you worry about grades or the sport you play or whether you will be accepted by your peers. When you pray, put your list before God. Pray over the things on your list and ask God to help you release all of your cares to him.

Wendy

Great Pyrenees

Group: Working

Size: 25 to 32 inches; 85 to 115 pounds

Origin: Great Pyrenees, often called Pyrs, are one of the oldest breeds in the world, dating all the way back to the tenth century. Originally, Pyrs were bred to guard sheep in the Pyrenees Mountains. In 1933 the Great Pyrenees received AKC recognition.[1]

Though the Great Pyrenees has won Best of Breed a few times at Westminster, no Pyr has ever won Best in Show as of 2023.

AKC: 1933

Night Guard

Great Pyrenees are naturally nocturnal. They are wired that way because, back in the day, they had to protect their assigned sheep each night while the shepherds slept. Pyrs also have a very keen sense of hearing and pretty impressive night vision, and their instinct to guard and protect is strong. This means they will bark a lot, at everything, all night. It's their job to be on guard, and they take it very seriously.

You know who else looks out for you all night—never sleeping or taking His eyes off of you? God! Psalm 121:4 assures us of that. And so does Proverbs 15:3. Isn't that amazing? I find it so comforting that God is looking out for me 24/7. We can count on Him to always be there, keeping His promises and watching over us. And He doesn't do it out of obligation. He watches over us because He loves us so much. So, sleep well tonight. You're being watched... in a good way.

Unleash the Truth: "He won't let you stumble, your Guardian God won't fall asleep. Not on your life! Israel's Guardian will never doze or sleep." (Psalm 121:3–4 MSG)

Digging Deeper: Do you ever have trouble sleeping? What keeps you awake at night? Next time you can't sleep, remember this scripture: "You can go to bed without fear; you will lie down and sleep soundly." (Proverbs 3:24 NLT)

Fido 411: The Great Pyrenees was once known as the royal dog of France.

Weekly Tail-Waggers: Pray this tonight before you go to sleep: "Father God, thank You for watching over me all day and all night. Help me trust You more so that I can sleep more soundly. I give my fears and worries to You. Thank You, Lord, for filling my dreams with Your peace and love. Amen."

Michelle

Greyhound

GROUP Hound

SIZE 27 to 30 inches; 60 to 70 pounds

ORIGIN Greyhounds have been around since ancient Egypt! About five thousand years ago, these dogs were the hunting partners of pharaohs. Ever since ancient times, they've been preferred companions for nobles and royalty.

Gia the Greyhound won Best in Show at the Purina National Dog Show in 2016 with her quick paws, beautiful figure, and shining personality.[1] But a Greyhound has never won Best in Show at Westminster.

AKC 1885

Deceptive Appearances

Greyhounds are known for their uniquely curved bodies and short, smooth fur. But Greyhounds are best known for being the world's fastest dog breed. They might not be what you would expect, though! In fact, the breed has been called the "forty-mile-per-hour couch potato"! That's because Greyhounds only have short bursts of energy, and for the rest of the day, they're completely content to sleep on the couch.

Most people assume that because Greyhounds are the fastest dogs, they would prefer to run all day. But that's not the case. It just goes to show you that you can't know what someone likes or understand how they are wired just by looking at them! And, it's always a bad idea to assume something about a person based on partial information or appearances.

We have to keep these things in mind when meeting new people too!

You may see a person with perfectly styled hair and brand-new clothes and assume that person's life is perfect when, in reality, she struggles with low self-esteem. Or you may see someone wearing clothing from a different culture and assume that person doesn't speak English—only to learn he speaks English perfectly, as well as five other languages!

How often do we come to the wrong conclusions about people based on how we perceive them at first, just like the Greyhound? It's important to get the real story before making judgments. Everyone deserves a chance to be understood, and the better we understand people, the better we can get along with them.

Unleash the Truth: "Look beneath the surface so you can judge correctly." (John 7:24 NLT)

Digging Deeper: Have you ever assumed something about someone based only on what you could see? How would you feel if someone made assumptions about you based on your appearance?

Fido 411: In addition to being companions of pharaohs and nobles, Greyhounds have been loyal sidekicks to General George A. Custer and President Rutherford B. Hayes.

Weekly Tail-Waggers: Have a conversation with someone today that you may have judged unfairly before. Compare and contrast what you thought about that person versus what is actually true. You might just be surprised.

Michelle

Ibizan Hound
(i-BEE-zun)

GROUP Hound

SIZE 22.5 to 27.5 inches; 45 to 50 pounds

ORIGIN The Ibizan Hound is an ancient dog named for an island in the Mediterranean off the coast of Spain. Images of the dog have been discovered in the tombs of Egyptian Pharaohs dating back to 3400 BC.[1]

The Ibizan Hound first appeared at the Westminster Dog Show in 1980. It has taken the top spot in the Hound group twice. The most recent win was in 2004.[2] The Ibizan also competes in lure coursing, obedience, agility, rally, and tracking.[3]

AKC 1978

You Can Leap Over Walls

The Ibizan Hound is a lanky rabbit hunter that uses deerlike ears, sharp vision, and a good nose to make it a triple threat. Their athletic build allows them to navigate the tall brush on their native islands with speed. And they have a special talent too. They can jump a good five or six feet into the air, easily clearing any obstacles in their way.[4]

For the Ibizan, obstacles are physical things like brush, fences, and walls. For Christian believers, our obstacles are anything that gets in the way of our purpose in life. They're like imaginary walls. They are walls that block God's blessing for us and keep us from achieving all the things God has planned for us to do. Sometimes the obstacles are relatively small. They make things a little harder, but we can still manage. But other walls can cause us to come to a screeching halt. We can't get around them or over them without help.

The great news is—we can get over *any* wall with God's help. We can do *all* things through Christ who gives us strength. It doesn't matter what our

Paws-itive Inspirations

wall is. It doesn't matter how big or how small we are, how smart or talented, how healthy or what physical problems we may have. Through Christ, God can, and will, help us overcome any obstacle in our path.

David fought many battles in his lifetime. He had to run for his life from King Saul. But through it all, God protected him and gave him victory. David joyously praised God for all he was able to accomplish by God's strength. He was fully convinced there was *nothing* he couldn't do with God's help—even run through an entire army or leap over a wall.

The same is true for every believer. We *can* do all things through Christ. We can leap over the walls in our lives like they are nothing. Not because *we* can but because God can.

Unleash the Truth: "For by You I can run against a troop; By my God I can leap over a wall." (2 Samuel 22:30 NKJV)

"I can do all things through Christ who strengthens me." (Philippians 4:13 NKJV)

"'Not by might nor by power, but by my Spirit,' says the Lord Almighty." (Zechariah 4:6)

Digging Deeper: What are the walls in your life?

Fido 411: An Ibizan Hound in Arkansas is a multitalented dog. Pepper is a Grand Champion and holds a paw full of other titles too. But her most important accomplishment is that of service dog to her owner, a retired Army veteran who suffers from Post-Traumatic Stress Disorder (PTSD).[5]

Weekly Tail-Waggers: As you think about the walls in your life, ask God to help you get over them. Maybe you're really shy and that keeps you from sharing your faith. Maybe you have trouble in school. Maybe your home life isn't the greatest. Whatever your wall, know that God can help you leap over it and into the blessing that comes from living your life for Him.

Wendy

Irish Setter

GROUP Sporting

SIZE 25 to 27 inches; 60 to 70 pounds

ORIGIN In the 1800s, Irish hunters bred Irish Setters to help them sniff out and retrieve the birds they'd hunted.

Irish Setters have competed in dog shows since the 1870s, and they've won the Sporting group competition eleven times at Westminster! But they have never won Best in Show.

AKC 1878

Obedience Lessons

Irish Setters are super sweet and very outgoing. But they are also known for being a little destructive when they get bored. If their owners leave them for more than a few hours, they can get upset and act out by chewing something (like your new tennis shoes!) or barking nonstop. And, if they weren't trained properly from a young age, it can be really hard for them to unlearn bad habits![1]

They're beautiful dogs and great companions, but they're stubborn pups for sure. They need consistent and strict training in order to make them good dogs—otherwise they'll start running wild!

When we start out on our path of being Christians, we can often be a lot like Irish Setters. We sometimes act out and get into trouble, especially when we feel left alone. Without guidance from God or our Christian friends, we may start running wild or return to the bad habits we learned before we became Christians. That's why God gives us rules, boundaries, and discipline. He loves us and wants us to be the best we can be. He wants to keep us safe.

Let's not be destructive like Irish Setters when we become frustrated or bored. Let's follow God's training and be patient, kind, and obedient. No matter how long you've been a Christian, there's always more to learn and ways to grow. And we have the best Teacher and the most amazing manual (the Bible) to help us become the very best we can be! Yay!

Unleash the Truth: "Sensible people control their temper; they earn respect by overlooking wrongs." (Proverbs 19:11 NLT)

Digging Deeper: What do you find yourself doing when you feel frustrated or alone? How can you respond in a better way that would please God?

Fido 411: The Irish Setter was one of the first nine dog breeds to be registered with the American Kennel Club.

Weekly Tail-Waggers: In your journal, make a list of things that make you feel most frustrated. Then write down how you can handle each situation by following God's rules and doing things His way.

Michelle

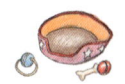

Irish Wolfhound

Group: Hound

Size: 30 to 32 inches; 105 to 120 pounds

Origin: The Irish Wolfhound is an ancient breed, and its true origins are lost in time. It is said that Julius Caesar returned to Rome from the British Isles with two such dogs, which he proudly displayed in his victory parade. Today the breed is considered a symbol of Irish culture.

The Wolfhound has frequently placed in its group at the Westminster Dog Show since its first appearance there in 1879. Originally a competitor in the sporting group, the Wolfhound was moved to the hound group in 1930.

AKC: 1897

Be Slow to Anger

Bred to hunt large prey like wolves, wild boar, elk, and deer, the Irish Wolfhound was fast enough to catch them and large enough to bring them down. They were so good at it, big game disappeared almost completely from Ireland, Scotland, and Northern Britain by the early 1800s.

In spite of their history as big game hunters, today's Wolfhounds are known for their amiable personality. They are true gentle giants that thrive in the company of family. In general, they are friendly to everyone, including strangers, as long as the strangers don't pose a threat to family members. It takes a lot to get a Wolfhound's "Irish up." You could say they're "slow to anger."

Being "slow to anger" is a quality God desires to see in us. We live in a time when people seem to explode in anger over every little thing. In fact, the Bible tells us in 2 Timothy 3 that one of the signs of the last days before Jesus returns is a lack of self-control. But the Bible also tells us that uncontrolled anger can give Satan a foothold, a starting point for taking over other parts of our lives too. And that is never a good thing.

In Galatians 5, the apostle Paul lists more than a dozen actions that can keep us from inheriting the kingdom of God. Among them is anger. Instead, Paul tells us, we are to live by the spirit of God. Giving in to anger causes us to lose control, a sign that we are not living as a Christian should.

Unleash the Truth: "He who is slow to anger is better than the powerful. And he who rules his spirit is better than he who takes a city." (Proverbs 16:32 NLV)

"And 'don't sin by letting anger control you.' Don't let the sun go down while you are still angry, for anger gives a foothold to the devil." (Ephesians 4:26–27 NLT)

Digging Deeper: Think about how you respond to anger. While there are legitimate reasons to be angry, your response to them is what counts. It's OK to be angry. Especially over an unfair situation or when someone deliberately hurts you. It's not OK to lose control. What you do or say when you are angry is 100 percent on you.

Fido 411: The Irish Wolfhound is the tallest of all the dog breeds. They stand thirty-two inches or more at the shoulder, and many can reach more than seven feet standing on their hind legs!

Weekly Tail-Waggers: If you have trouble with losing control when you are angry, ask God to help you. You can pray, "Father, I know that I have a problem when I lose my temper. I know that's not what You want to see in me, and I don't want to allow my anger to control me. Please help me exercise self-control and keep me from giving Satan a foothold in my life. In Jesus' name. Amen."

Wendy

Japanese Chin

Group: Toy

Size: 8 to 11 inches tall; 7 to 11 pounds

Origin: Although its name has "Japanese" in it, it's believed the Japanese Chin originated in China or Korea. There are several theories as to how they got to Japan, including by way of Buddhist monks or Korean royalty.[1]

The Japanese Chin has not won the top prize at Westminster or AKC.

The Japanese Chin was recognized in 1888 as the Japanese Spaniel. The name was changed in 1977 to the Japanese Chin.

Celebrate Who You Are!

Japanese Chin are adorable, little "indoorsy" dogs with a history that boasts of royalty, and they must know it by the way they carry themselves. This beautiful breed has a rather large head for its body with a short snout and round eyes that make them look like they are always surprised. A Chin's coat can be either black and white, red, orange, lemon, sable and white, or black and white with tan spots over each eye, inside the ears, and on both cheeks. No matter their color, these little dogs are very cute—and catlike.

Yep, that's right, catlike. The Chin has an uncanny ability to jump onto high perches such as fireplace mantles, the backs of couches, and tall bookshelves much like a kitty! This breed also grooms itself much like a cat, licking its paws and wiping its head. It's been known to bat at objects during playtime, much like a cat would play. It's no wonder this little dog is friendly to felines. In fact, the Japanese Chin gets along with most everyone and has a very happy way about it.

One could imagine that other dog breeds might not understand why Chins are so catlike or why they are so friendly to felines, but you know what? It's OK to be different. It's OK for the Chin to stand out from the rest of the canine crowd. And, guess what. It's OK for us too!

The Bible tells us that when we give our lives to God, we become new creatures. In John 17:14, it says that we are no longer of this world, meaning we probably won't fit in with the world's way of thinking once we make Jesus Lord over our lives. The world won't understand us or even like us at times because of our beliefs, but we can't let that affect how we live our lives. Just keep being a Christian, doing the right thing, and following what the Bible says—no matter what. And, like the Japanese Chin, you'll have a happy heart.

Unleash the Truth: "I have given them your word. And the world hates them because they do not belong to the world, just as I do not belong to the world. I'm not asking you to take them out of the world, but to keep them safe from the evil one. They do not belong to this world any more than I do. Make them holy by your truth; teach them your word, which is truth." (John 17:14–17 NLT)

Digging Deeper: Have you ever been treated badly because you stood up for your Christian beliefs? How did that make you feel? Would you stand up for your beliefs again, knowing you might be made fun of or rejected because of your faith?

Fido 411: Did you know that Chin owners say their dogs don't really bark but rather chatter? Chins often "sing" to announce to their owners that strangers are approaching.[2]

Weekly Tail-Waggers: Grab your journal and write down a few characteristics about yourself that make you feel different. Maybe you are the only one in your family who likes a certain sports team, or maybe you prefer camping while the rest of your family is indoorsy. Celebrate who you are, and more important, celebrate who God created you to be!

Michelle

Keeshond
(KAYZ-hund)

GROUP   Non-Sporting

SIZE   17 to 18 inches; 35 to 45 pounds

ORIGIN   Although descended from ancient spitz-type dogs (northern sled dogs), the Keeshond was developed in Holland and Germany. They were known for being watchdogs and companions on barges and freight carriers.[1]

The Keeshond regularly places in the Non-Sporting group at Westminster, including a win in 1968.[2] Keeshonden (the plural of Keeshond) do well in a variety of other events including agility, lure coursing, and herding, and they also make wonderful therapy dogs.[3]

AKC   1930

The Company You Keep

Keeshond literally means Kees's dog. One of the leaders of a Patriot movement in Belgium (attempting to overthrow the ruling class during the 1780s) was named Cornelis (Kees) de Gijselaar. Kees's dog was a barge dog, a working dog, who came to represent the working man and the cause of the Patriots. The Patriots identified themselves by wearing badges showing the dog.

Kees's dog was known to all by the company he kept. He was associated with the Patriot movement, and everyone who saw him knew him as part of the rebellion. Everything was fine until the Patriots were defeated. Then it was no longer safe to wear a badge with Kees's dog on it. In fact, it wasn't even safe to own a dog that looked like him. Although the name Keeshond remained, the breed almost disappeared. No one wanted to own a dog that might make the rulers think they had also been part of the rebellion.[4]

Paws-itive Inspirations

We know that Kees's dog wasn't responsible for anything his owner did—whether it was right or wrong. But this story does show us something that is true for everyone no matter what century you live in. We are known by the company we keep. If we hang out with and associate with people who are known for doing good, then we will be thought of as someone who does good things too. And if we hang out with people who cause trouble and do bad things, then people will think the same of us.

And there's something else. One of the characteristics of human nature is that we become like those we associate with. There's an old saying: bad company corrupts good morals. And it's true. When a person hangs out with people who have a bad attitude (or worse), it isn't long before they have that same attitude. It can work the other way too. When a person chooses to associate with positive people, they can't help but be positive themselves. It matters who your friends are because you *are* who you hang out with.

Unleash the Truth: "Walk with the wise and become wise, for a companion of fools suffers harm." (Proverbs 13:20)

"Do not make friends with a hot-tempered person, do not associate with one easily angered, or you may learn their ways and get yourself ensnared." (Proverbs 22:24–25)

Digging Deeper: Do you have friends who encourage you in your faith?

Fido 411: The Keeshond is also known as the Smiling Dutchman. Their smiling expression goes well with their happy, easygoing personality.[5]

Weekly Tail-Waggers: This week give some serious thought to the people with whom you spend the most time. Remember, you can't choose your family, but you *can* choose your friends. Choose wisely. Choose to associate with people who will encourage you to be the best person and Christian you can be.

Wendy

Komondor

(kuh-MAHN-dor)

GROUP — Working

SIZE — 25.5 to 27.5 inches; 80 to 100 pounds

ORIGIN — The true origin of the Komondor is not known, but it was most likely developed by the Cumans—a nomadic people originally from Central Asia. In the 1200s they migrated to central Hungary where they bred the Komondor as a livestock guard dog.[1]

The Komondor took Best in Group at Westminster in 1993. They have placed in that group five other times but have never taken a Best in Show. Komondors do compete in other types of events but are not known for frequent wins.[2]

AKC — 1937

Guard Your Heart

The Komondor is one very unique-looking dog. Maybe you've seen them in commercials on television. They look like a giant mop. And because they aren't common in our country, seeing one in real life is a treat.

Most of the time, the Komondor is a gentle giant. They're mostly calm and very reserved toward strangers. And, as you might imagine, something that looks like a big mop doesn't appear very scary. But if a Komondor senses a threat to his property or family all that calm can change in an instant. Because they are such large, powerful dogs, they are able to swiftly and effectively deal with intruders or predators. At the first hint that something is off, they jump into action to guard the people, property, or animals in their care.

The Komondor's instinct to guard is a lesson for believers. The Bible tells us we are to guard our hearts, and we should do so with the same determination as a Komondor. That's because everything we do is guided by our hearts. And wherever our focus and affections are—our heart will be. We have to make sure our heart is always in the right place and that we pursue the right things.

That's sounds simple enough, right? But the problem is that our hearts can lead us astray. If our focus is on getting the things the world has to offer (money, fame, power, having lots of stuff), then our hearts will be corrupted by those things. Instead, the Bible tells us, we should work to store up treasures in heaven. Guarding our heart means making sure that our focus is on God and not the world. And when our focus is on Him, our lives will just naturally honor Him, and our hearts will be in the *right* place.

Unleash the Truth: "Above all else, guard your heart, for everything you do flows from it." (Proverbs 4:23)

"The heart is deceitful above all things and beyond cure. Who can understand it?" (Jeremiah 17:9)

"For where your treasure is, there your heart will be also." (Matthew 6:21)

Digging Deeper: What are the things (treasures) you desire most?

Fido 411: During World War II, Komondors were often used as guard dogs for military posts. So many were killed in service that the breed almost died out completely.[3]

Weekly Tail-Waggers: Spend some time examining your heart this week. Is your focus on the right things? Are your treasures stored up in heaven? Make it a habit to check your heart often. Ask God to help you keep your focus on the things that matter to Him, and your heart will always be in great shape.

Wendy

Labradoodle

GROUP Crossbreed

SIZE *standard*—21 to 24 inches; 50 to 65 pounds, *medium*—17 to 20 inches; 30 to 45 pounds, *miniature*—14 to 16 inches; 15 to 25 pounds[1]

ORIGIN The development of Labradoodles as a breed began in Australia. A breeder at Guide Dogs Victoria mated a Poodle with a Labrador Retriever after receiving a request for a guide dog that was hypoallergenic. The resulting dog had a wonderful temperament and the required nonirritating coat.[2]

Although Labradoodles do not compete in AKC events, they excel as guide dogs, service dogs, and therapy dogs.[3]

AKC The Labradoodle is not recognized by the AKC.

Our Anchor Holds

Labradoodles vary in size depending on the parent dogs. They have either a tightly curled wool coat or a loosely curled fleece coat. No matter which one a Labradoodle has, they usually don't shed. That means they're a good dog for people with allergies.[4]

Because Labradoodles are both smart and amiable, they make great service dogs. They are especially good dogs for children and adults on the autism spectrum. Labradoodles quickly learn to sense when their owner is getting overwhelmed and can either redirect the person's attention or provide deep tissue therapy by lying on top of them. Some families use Labradoodles (or other service dogs) as a kind of anchor to keep little ones with autism from wandering off. A child on the spectrum who gets separated from family often can't communicate. This makes routine activities difficult for families who don't have a service dog to help.[5]

A Labradoodle provides stability and a calming presence for someone on the autism spectrum. In the same way, God is always with us too. He promises that He will never leave us or forsake us. That's something we can hold on to! Even when things get choppy and we find ourselves being blown around by the winds of life, we have an anchor that keeps us steady. The hope we have in Jesus is like an anchor for our souls. And it will hold in any storm.

Unleash the Truth: "So God has given both his promise and his oath. These two things are unchangeable because it is impossible for God to lie. Therefore, we who have fled to him for refuge can have great confidence as we hold to the hope that lies before us. This hope is a strong and trustworthy anchor for our souls. It leads us through the curtain into God's inner sanctuary." (Hebrews 6:18–19 NLT)

Digging Deeper: Just because you are a Christian doesn't mean you will never have anything bad happen to you. We live in a world full of sin. Stuff happens. Sometimes we make bad decisions. But no matter what, know this: our Christian hope is a sure thing. Just hold on to Him.

Fido 411: Although Labradoodles were developed as a breed in Australia, other people had the idea of crossing a Poodle with a Labrador too. One was a famous British race-car driver and boat racer named Donald Campbell, who set land and water speed records in the 1950s and 1960s. His favorite dog, Maxie, was a Poodle Lab mix born in 1949—long before the development of Labradoodles in Australia.[6]

Weekly Tail-Waggers: Think about this: God cannot and will not break His promises. And so, when He promises to be with us always, you can be sure He will. When things get tough, hang on to Him. He'll never let you go!

Wendy

Labrador Retriever

GROUP Sporting

SIZE 21.5 to 24.5 inches; 55 to 80 pounds

ORIGIN Labrador Retrievers were used primarily to help hunters catch ducks and fish on the island of Newfoundland. They were brought to England in the 1800s and have now become the most popular dog breed in America.

Though they've been America's favorite dog breed for more than twenty-five years, a Labrador Retriever has never won the Best in Show at the Westminster Dog Show.[1] But in 2020, a Black Lab named Heart won the Westminster Masters Obedience Championship for the fifth time in a row![2]

AKC 1917

Help Is on the Way

Yellow Labs, Black Labs, Chocolate Labs—they're all beloved pets, and they're all known for being friendly and helpful. If there are any Labradors in your life, you probably know them for their sweet personalities and fluffy wagging tails.

Labrador Retrievers were originally bred as fishermen's helpers; their job was to haul nets, fetch ropes, and retrieve fish in the chilly North Atlantic Sea. While some still have fishing gigs, most Labradors today help people in other ways. They are often trained to help guide blind people, comfort those with mental health struggles, or perform tasks to aid those with physical disabilities. Many Labradors are even trained to sense health problems in their owner and seek another person for assistance when needed. (Some can even sense when their owners are going to have a seizure and get them to a safe place.)

In the same way that Labradors are bred to help people, God made us with a deep desire to help others. We're wired to serve people, and, when we know how much God loves us, that gives us even more motivation to offer our assistance when possible. The more time you spend talking to God and paying attention to everything He has done for you, the more excited you'll be to share His love with others! Like outgoing Labradors, let's serve our Master with enthusiasm and help His people as best as we can! You may not have a tail to wag, but let the joy of serving others bubble out of your heart.

Unleash the Truth: "Trust in the Lord and do good; dwell in the land and enjoy safe pasture." (Psalm 37:3)

Digging Deeper: How can you offer help to the people you see every day? How can you reach outside of your normal circle and lend a hand? Maybe you could volunteer to rake your neighbor's leaves or work as a vacation Bible school helper!

Fido 411: One litter of Retrievers can have all three colors of Labs in it![3]

Weekly Tail-Waggers: Choose three ways you can help others today. They can be as big or as little as you want! You can do anything from helping your mom wash the dishes to starting a food drive for people who don't have any food in your community.

Michelle

Lhasa Apso

Group Non-Sporting

Size 10 to 11 inches; 12 to 18 pounds

Origin The Lhasa Apso is an ancient breed from Tibet. It is linked with palaces and Buddhist monasteries as well as with the Dalai Lama. It is known for its thick coat of hair and a tail that curls up over its back.

This long-haired beauty has never won Best in Show at Westminster or taken top honors at the American Kennel Club, but it has won a lot of hearts all over the world.

AKC The Lhasa Apso was first registered in 1935 in the Terrier group but was reassigned to the Non-Sporting group in 1959.

Who Doesn't Like a Gift?

Lhasa Apsos are such pretty little pooches that they used to be given as very special gifts in Tibet. In fact, if you received a Lhasa as a present, it was considered a sign that you'd have good fortune. According to historic retellings, the Dalai Lama once gave a Lhasa to the emperor of China many centuries ago, and that led to the beginnings of the related breed of the Shih Tzu.

You know who else likes to give good gifts? Your heavenly Father, that's who! In the Bible (Matthew 7:11), it says: "If you, then, though you are evil, know how to give good gifts to your children, how much more will your Father in heaven give good gifts to those who ask him!"

You see, God wants to bless His children, and that means us! So, don't be afraid to ask God for things you desire because here's the scoop: if you have a strong desire in your heart, chances are God put it there! For example, if you've always desired to be a writer, go for it and ask your heavenly Father to help you fulfill that dream. Ask Him to open doors for you that no person can shut! He will! He's a good God and He knows how to give good gifts—gifts even better than a Lhasa Apso. So, go ahead. Ask Him!

Unleash the Truth: "Every good and perfect gift is from above, coming down from the Father of the heavenly lights, who does not change like shifting shadows." (James 1:17)

Digging Deeper: How does it make you feel when you give someone a gift? Sometimes it's just as fun to *give* a gift as it is to *receive* one, isn't it?

Fido 411: Did you know Lhasa is the name of Tibet's sacred city, and Apso means "longhaired dog"?

Weekly Tail-Waggers: Gifts don't always have to cost money. Giving someone a homemade card or even a smile can be the best gift of all. Maybe you can give several of those kinds of gifts to the people in your life today!

Michelle

Maltese

Group: Toy

Size: 7 to 9 inches; under 7 pounds

Origin: The Maltese comes from an island called Malta in the Mediterranean Sea. They were the favorite pets of royalty in the Roman empire!

In 2014, a Maltese named Kiwi won Best in Show at the National Owner-Handler Series Finals but it has never won Best in Show at Westminster.

AKC: 1888

Furry and Friendly

You'll recognize a Maltese right away because of its long, straight white hair. Beneath all that fur is a tiny little body that's full of affection and helpfulness. Maltese are friendly and gentle with everyone they meet, which is why they make great therapy dogs! And, despite their miniature size, they love to be watchdogs because they are fearless in defending the people they love.

We can learn a thing or two from these tiny pooches! Maltese have so many great qualities that God wants us to have, like happiness, kindness, faithfulness, and gentleness. In the same way that Maltese want to make sure everyone around them is comfortable and safe, we can help the people around us by loving and defending them. God is so pleased when we find joy in helping His children! As Christians, we can be like the Maltese by being the loving, sweet, friendly people who light up the room just by being in it!

Let's take a lesson from these kindhearted canines and be friendly, kind, and helpful!

Unleash the Truth: "But the fruit of the Spirit is love, joy, peace, forbearance, kindness, goodness, faithfulness, gentleness and self-control." (Galatians 5:22–23).

Digging Deeper: Take a look at the Bible verse above. Which of those "fruits" do you think you have? Which ones do you think you might need more of?

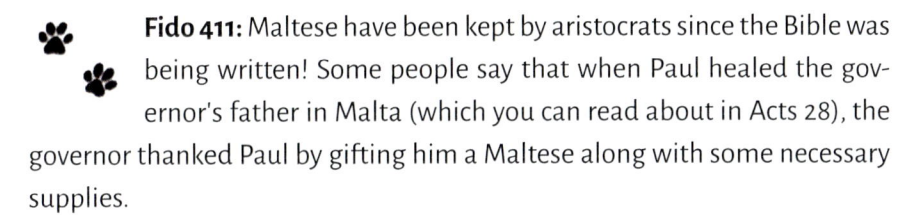

Fido 411: Maltese have been kept by aristocrats since the Bible was being written! Some people say that when Paul healed the governor's father in Malta (which you can read about in Acts 28), the governor thanked Paul by gifting him a Maltese along with some necessary supplies.

Weekly Tail-Waggers: Choose one of the "fruits" from Galatians 5:22–23 that you would like to develop more. In your journal, write a list of ways you can go out of your way to use that fruit this week. When you try the things on your list, write down how it went. You'll be amazed at how you grow!

Michelle

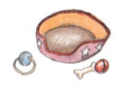

Maremma Sheepdog

GROUP Working

SIZE 25.5 to 28.5 inches; 66 to 99 pounds[1]

ORIGIN Maremmas were bred centuries ago by the sheep farmers of Italy's central plains to watch over their flocks.

Maremmas are rarely seen in dog shows or obedience competitions. However, a program using Maremmas to protect an endangered species of penguin received an award from the Australian government in 2010.[2]

AKC The Maremma Sheepdog is not recognized by the AKC.

Someone to Watch Over You

Maremma sheepdogs are known for their abilities as livestock guard dogs. They are smart and can think on their feet. They protect their flocks from four-legged predators, like wolves, and from two-legged thieves at all costs. To a Maremma—the flock is family.[3]

In a human family, the dad is often the protector. And even when there isn't a dad to take that role, there is usually someone in the family who tries to keep everyone else safe. It's a wonderful feeling to know that someone loves you and is watching over you.

But what if you have no family? Or what if no one in your human family cares enough to watch over you?

Sometimes the world is a scary place. But no matter what situation we find ourselves in or what our earthly family may be like, we can be sure of one thing: our heavenly Father is always watching out for us. The Bible says He even sends angels to stand guard over us and protect us. Isn't that amazing? The same God who created the universe loves us and is always watching out for us. That's a comforting thought. And because God's got our back, we don't have to be afraid. He is always with us.

Unleash the Truth: "For he will order his angels to protect you wherever you go." (Psalm 91:11 NLT)

"The Lord will keep you from all harm—he will watch over your life; the Lord will watch over your coming and going both now and forevermore." (Psalm 121:7–8)

Digging Deeper: The Bible tells us fear is not from God. If fear is not from God, where do you think it comes from?

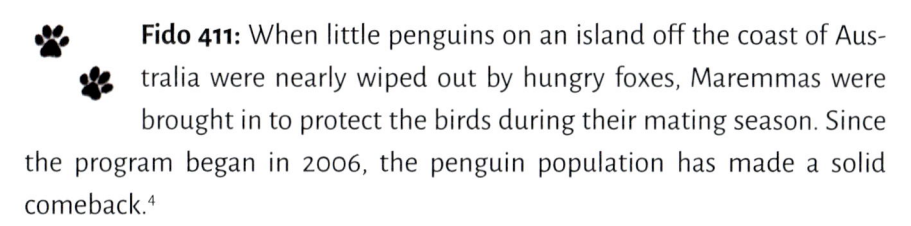

Fido 411: When little penguins on an island off the coast of Australia were nearly wiped out by hungry foxes, Maremmas were brought in to protect the birds during their mating season. Since the program began in 2006, the penguin population has made a solid comeback.[4]

Weekly Tail-Waggers: 2 Timothy 1:7 is a great verse to learn by heart. Then, whenever you are afraid you can say out loud, "God has not given us a spirit of fear and timidity, but of power, love, and self-discipline." (NLT)

Wendy

Mixed Breed

GROUP — Varies according to dominant characteristics

SIZE — Varies according to mixture of breeds

ORIGIN — Anywhere

Many mixed-breed dogs compete in obedience and agility trials and other types of canine competitions. They also make excellent therapy pets.[1]

AKC — Mixed breeds are not recognized by the AKC.

Best Adoption Ever!

A mixed breed dog doesn't have a set of papers to verify its bloodline. It's just a genetic mishmash of its parents and grandparents. The results aren't always the prettiest dog, but they're usually some of the best. Some people wouldn't want to own anything else, but others just think of them as mutts.

In New Testament days, many Jewish people felt that same way about non-Jewish people. As far as they were concerned, the Gentiles were like mixed breed dogs—mutts. Then God called a man named Saul (who became Paul) to carry the message of the gospel to the Gentiles. At first, many of Jesus' followers couldn't believe it! They thought salvation was meant for only the Jews. But God showed them that He intended to save the whole world through His son, Jesus. The Israelites (Jewish people) were God's chosen people. But because God loved *all* the people of the world so much, He sent Jesus to die for the sins of the whole world.

What does that mean for us? If we are believers, it means we've been adopted into the family of God! Through our faith in Jesus Christ, the Bible says we gain all the rights and privileges of a son or daughter. The creator of the universe becomes our Father! And this makes us heirs, along with God's chosen people (Israel), to the promises we have in Christ Jesus. It doesn't matter if we aren't purebreds. What matters is that we belong to Him.

Unleash the Truth: "For God did not send his Son into the world to condemn the world, but to save the world through him." (John 3:17)

"This mystery is that through the gospel the Gentiles are heirs together with Israel, members together of one body, and sharers together in the promise in Christ Jesus." (Ephesians 3:6)

"The Spirit you received does not make you slaves, so that you live in fear again; rather, the Spirit you received brought about your adoption to sonship. And by him we cry, '*Abba*, Father.' The Spirit himself testifies with our spirit that we are God's children." (Romans 8:15–16)

Digging Deeper: How do you view God? Do you see Him as your heavenly Father?

Fido 411: Mixed breed dogs are usually healthier than purebreds. They are less likely to inherit genetic disorders or to pass them on to their offspring.[2]

Weekly Tail-Waggers: With the help of a family member, create a family tree. Put in the names of your grandparents, your parents, and your siblings. And at the top of your family tree be sure to put God as your heavenly Father.

Wendy

Newfoundland

GROUP Working

SIZE 26 to 28 inches; 100 to 150 pounds

ORIGIN The Newfoundland's exact origin is unknown, although they are usually associated with the Canadian province of the same name. They have long held a reputation for being excellent deckhands and fearless water rescuers.[1]

The Newfoundland has taken Best in Show at Westminster twice. It regularly places in its Working group.[2]

AKC 1886

Found!

Newfoundlands are as much at home in the water as they are on land. They were originally used by fishermen to retrieve nets. But their strength and swimming ability has also made them awesome water rescue dogs. They're famous for rescuing kids in danger, especially in the water.[3]

In the early 1800s a Newfoundland named Seaman was part of the famous Lewis and Clark Expedition to explore the Louisiana Purchase and the Oregon Territory. Seaman belonged to Meriwether Lewis and served as the group's companion and guide. He hauled supplies, guarded the camp, and sometimes even provided food for the group.[4] He was one smart dog!

At one point Seaman was kidnapped by the Chinook Indians. The Chinooks were so impressed with Seaman that they wanted to keep him. Lewis sent out a search party. Their orders were to find Seaman and bring him back—no matter what.[5]

Seaman was very valuable to Lewis. He was prepared to keep on searching until Seaman was found. And the Bible says that Jesus is prepared to do the same for us.

In Luke 15 Jesus tells a parable about a man who had one hundred sheep. One of the sheep was lost, so the man left the ninety-nine and searched until he found it. The man was so overjoyed to find his lost sheep he threw a party. In the same way, Jesus said, all of heaven rejoices when even one sinner is saved.

Today, Jesus is looking for sinners who are like lost sheep. He wants *all* of us to be in the safety of his fold. He wants us to spend eternity with him. The question for you is: Are you already in the fold? Or are you still lost? Do you know Jesus as your personal savior? If not, he's looking for you. And he wants you to come home.

Unleash the Truth: "Then Jesus told them this parable: 'Suppose one of you has a hundred sheep and loses one of them. Doesn't he leave the ninety-nine in the open country and go after the lost sheep until he finds it? And when he finds it, he joyfully puts it on his shoulders and goes home. Then he calls his friends and neighbors together and says, "Rejoice with me; I have found my lost sheep." I tell you that in the same way there will be more rejoicing in heaven over one sinner who repents than over ninety-nine righteous persons who do not need to repent.'" (Luke 15:3–7)

Digging Deeper: Are you a lost sheep? Or have you been found by Jesus?

Fido 411: One of the things that makes Newfoundlands such great swimmers is their webbed feet. Just like a duck, only better! Their strong, webbed feet let them travel easily over land (not like a duck) and move quickly in the water.[6]

Weekly Tail-Waggers: If you have never made Jesus the Lord of your life, you can do that right now by praying this prayer:

Dear Jesus, I know that I am a sinner. I'm lost. I can't find myself. Only You can do that. But I want to come home to You. I believe that You are the Son of God and the Savior of the world. I need You to save me. Please come into my heart and be the Lord of my life. Rescue me from my sins and give me eternal life. I ask this in Your name. Amen.

Wendy

Old English Sheepdog

GROUP Herding

SIZE 21 inches and up; 60 to 100 pounds

ORIGIN The Old English Sheepdog (OES) is neither old nor English nor a sheepdog. It dates back to the late 1700s in southwest England but is of Scottish, European, and Russian ancestry. It was bred as a "drover's dog" to drive cattle to market.[1]

The OES has been crowned Best in Show twice in its long history at Westminster and has placed in its group an amazing fifty-one times![2] The OES is versatile enough to compete in herding, agility, obedience, rally, tracking, and coursing events. They also make wonderful therapy dogs.[3]

AKC 1888

It's Going to Take Some Work

An Old English Sheepdog is a well-balanced, sweet-tempered herding dog built for power and endurance. They can take off in an instant, move with speed, and are able to execute quick turns. This allows them to skillfully move cattle over long distances on rough terrain. And while they're working in the field, their warning bark has a loud, distinctive ring to it making them easy to find.

But the OES's most distinguishing characteristic is their shaggy fur. Their trademark gray-and-white coat is a sight to behold when it is well-groomed. However, as OES owners know, keeping their pups looking nice takes at least three to four hours a week. It's a huge time commitment. The reward is a beautiful dog that's a real head turner.[4]

Some things are just worth the time investment. Time spent studying the Bible, prayer, and meditation on the Word are worth your time. These are things that will help you grow in Christ and build your faith.

From the moment we accept Jesus as Lord, we become Christians—followers of Jesus Christ. But being "born again" doesn't mean we automatically know everything we need to know to follow Jesus. We start out as baby Christians. To grow and mature we have to put in some work. It takes some effort on our part to become grown-up Christians, but the rewards are *so* worth it.

Unleash the Truth: "Do your best to present yourself to God as one approved, a worker who does not need to be ashamed and who correctly handles the word of truth." (2 Timothy 2:15)

"Whatever you do, work at it with all your heart, as working for the Lord, not for human masters, since you know that you will receive an inheritance from the Lord as a reward. It is the Lord Christ you are serving." (Colossians 3:23–24)

Digging Deeper: What kinds of activities are you doing this week that will help you grow in your faith?

Fido 411: In the 1800s it became customary to dock, or bob, the tail of an OES to show it was a working dog. Working dogs were exempt from taxes. As a result, the OES earned the nickname "Bobtail" or "Bob."[5]

Weekly Tail-Waggers: Make it a habit to read one chapter in your Bible every day. A Bible app can help you stay on track to meet your daily reading goals. Take a minute or two to think about what you have read. Ask God to help you understand and hold His Word in your heart so that you can live the life He wants you to live.

Wendy

Papillon
(PA-pee-ahn)

GROUP Toy

SIZE 8 to 11 inches; 5 to 10 pounds

ORIGIN Although *Papillon* is French for "butterfly," the origin of this breed is unknown. Descended from toy spaniels, the Papillon was a favorite in the royal courts of Western Europe in the 1600s and 1700s.[1]

The Papillon has competed at Westminster since 1906. It took Best in Show in 1999 and has placed an additional nine times.[2] Papillons do well in obedience, agility, and tracking competitions and are ideal therapy and service dogs.[3]

AKC 1915

Listen More, Talk Less

A Papillon is a small, outgoing little dog with a fun-loving personality. Originally bred to keep rats out of the home, they're smart and easily trained, which makes them great companion dogs. Their uniquely large, fringed ears fan out like butterfly wings. The French were quick to notice and dubbed them "Papillon."

The Papillon is a lot of dog in a small package. But if they have one fault it's that they aren't quite convinced of their own size. Papillons often exhibit what is known as "small dog syndrome." This can lead to aggressive behaviors like barking at, biting, and bullying much larger dogs. It seems the Papillon doesn't know when to keep its mouth shut.[4]

Knowing when to keep your mouth shut is a good thing for anyone to know. The Bible says we should be quick to listen and slow to speak.

Paws-itive Inspirations

Something said in the heat of the moment can lead to angry shouting and sometimes physical blows. But nothing is ever gained by getting into arguments and fighting. Worse, it does not reflect well on someone who claims to be a Christian.

You might think, since a Papillon has such big ears and such a tiny mouth, that it would be more likely to listen than bark. And you might think that since human beings have two ears and only one mouth, we'd listen more than we talk. Unfortunately, we humans aren't any better at controlling our mouths than a little Papillon. Learning to listen more and speak less requires self-discipline. It isn't natural, but it *can* be developed. Prayer and Bible study are two things that can help us with that. Both will help produce the righteousness God wants to see in us.

So, note to self: Listen more. Talk less. Grow in righteousness.

Unleash the Truth: "My dear brothers and sisters, take note of this: Everyone should be quick to listen, slow to speak and slow to become angry, because human anger does not produce the righteousness that God desires." (James 1:19–20)

Digging Deeper: Have you ever said something you wish you hadn't? Did saying it lead to anger on your part or someone else's?

Fido 411: Marie Antoinette was the last queen of France before the French Revolution. She owned many dogs, but her favorite was a Papillon named Coco. Rumor has it the queen walked to her own execution clutching her beloved pet.[5]

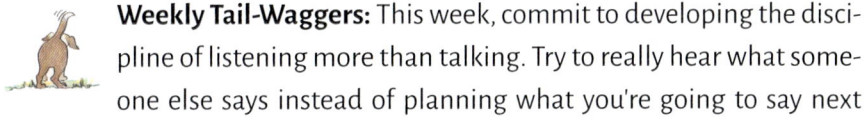

Weekly Tail-Waggers: This week, commit to developing the discipline of listening more than talking. Try to really hear what someone else says instead of planning what you're going to say next while they are still talking. Ask God to help you develop the righteousness He desires in you.

Wendy

Parson Russell Terrier

GROUP — Terrier

SIZE — 12 to 15 inches; 11 to 13 pounds

ORIGIN — The Parson Russell Terrier originated in England. It was one of several small, mostly white terriers bred by the Reverend John Russell as foxhunting dogs. Parsons traveled on foot with the hounds, which chased the fox underground if needed.[1]

The Parson Russell Terrier is relatively new to the Westminster Dog Show and has no awards there yet. However, their intelligence and stamina make them a natural for earthdog, companion, and course competitions. They are also especially good at agility and obedience competitions.

AKC — 1997

Fear Not!

Parson Russell Terriers aren't afraid of anything. They are small dogs with big courage. And they'll follow the animal they are chasing into an underground burrow without hesitation if needed. Why is that? Maybe they know their owners are almost always right behind. They know that even if the fight gets hard, they can trust their humans to be right there.

Sometimes life can feel like a daily fight. And there are often things that we *have* to face that are bigger than we are. And scary too. When we get to heaven, we won't have to worry about that. But for now, life can be filled with things that can cause fear.

There's that big test next week in your weakest subject. And there's that baseball tournament coming up with the league championship on the line.

What if you mess up? There's that bully in the grade ahead of you. He or she hasn't ever noticed you, but you're worried they might.

And then there's the really big stuff like earthquakes and storms and people getting sick everywhere. It's no wonder that many people live in fear. There's a lot to be scared of if you are looking at things from your own point of view.

That's why it's so important to know that your heavenly Father is *always* there. He's *with* you in every situation, no matter how scary. And He'll get you through it. *If* we trust God and decide that *he* is our safe place and *say* it out loud, the Bible says no harm will overtake us or come near where we live. Trust God. Make Him your safe place. And say it *out loud*. When we do this and keep our eyes on Him, we can know without any doubt that He is right there.

We have nothing to fear because our God is with us and helps us no matter what. He doesn't want us to be afraid. He wants us to trust Him. Fear not!

Unleash the Truth: "Fear not, for I am with you. Do not be dismayed. I am your God. I will strengthen you; I will help you; I will uphold you with my victorious right hand." (Isaiah 41:10 TLB)

Digging Deeper: What causes you to be afraid?

Fido 411: The Parson Russell Terrier is the taller cousin to the Russell Terrier. While Russells were meant to be carried in saddlebags on a hunt, the Parson's longer legs and higher energy level made them ideal for running with the hounds and horses.[2]

Weekly Tail-Waggers: Take time to read Psalm 91 this week. Know that God is your protector and hiding place. In your prayer time declare this:

Father, *You* are my refuge. I will live in *You*. Thank *You* for holding me up with *Your* mighty right hand. I will not be afraid. I will trust in *You*. Amen.

Wendy

Pekingese

GROUP Toy

SIZE 6 to 9 inches; up to 14 pounds

ORIGIN The ancient breed of Pekingese is closely related to the emperors of China. They were bred to look like miniature lions and became known as "Foo Dogs." They made their way to England in 1860 and into the United States by the early 1900s.[1]

A Pekingese named Wasabi won Best in Show at Westminster in 2021, which was the fifth time a Pekingese claimed the top honor. The last time was in 2012.

AKC 1906

Royal Through and Through

It's no wonder why Pekingese walk with their heads held high and a bit of swagger in their step. They know they belong in the palace; they know they were adored by emperors; they instinctively know they are royal. Hundreds of years may have passed since they were an important part of the royal families in China, but that attitude of knowing they are valuable runs deep in this breed.

Guess what? That same attitude should run deep in us, too, because we are royal! We are children of the King of Kings! Need more convincing? Well, 1 Peter 2:9 calls us "a royal priesthood." And, Revelation 1:6 says, "and has made us kings and priests to His God and Father, to Him be glory and dominion forever and ever. Amen" (NKJV). Also, Revelation 5:10 says, "You let them become kings and serve God as priests, and they will rule on earth" (CEV).

God has even given us crowns. Psalm 8:4–6 says, "What is man that You are mindful of him, And the son of man that You visit him? For You have made him a little lower than the angels, And You have crowned him with glory and honor" (NKJV).

You may not *feel* royal but you *are* royal. When you made Jesus the Lord of your life, you became born again, and that means you were born into a royal family! You became a child of the King of Kings! You see, it doesn't matter who you are. It only matters *Whose* you are. So, on those days when you are feeling less than royal, straighten that invisible crown and remind yourself who your Daddy is! Go ahead, put a little swagger in your step just like the Pekingese, knowing that you come from a royal bloodline.

Pray this with me:

Father, thank You for adopting me into Your family. Help me, Lord, to begin to see myself the way that You see me. I love You. In the mighty name of Your son, Jesus, amen.

Unleash the Truth: "But you are a chosen people, a royal priesthood, a holy nation, God's special possession, that you may declare the praises of him who called you out of darkness into his wonderful light." (1 Peter 2:9)

Digging Deeper: Do you feel special, or do you struggle with feeling like you're not good enough?

Fido 411: Did you know that this breed is known to snore rather loudly because of their short noses?[2]

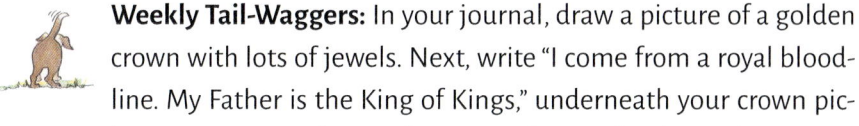

Weekly Tail-Waggers: In your journal, draw a picture of a golden crown with lots of jewels. Next, write "I come from a royal bloodline. My Father is the King of Kings," underneath your crown picture. Let this picture remind you of your royalty on the days when you're feeling less than crown worthy.

Michelle

Pembroke Welsh Corgi

Group: Herding

Size: 10 to 12 inches; 28 to 30 pounds

Origin: One of two breeds known as a Welsh Corgi, the Pembroke Welsh Corgi is from Pembrokeshire, Wales, where it was used as a cattle-herding dog.

Although this charming breed has never won Best in Show at Westminster, it has won Best of Group seven times![1]

AKC: 1934

Live to Serve, Aim to Please

Pembroke Welsh Corgis are happiest when they are being useful. All-around great farm dogs, they are able to move cattle from pasture to pasture by nipping at the cattle's heels. They are powerful, quick dogs with a great work ethic. As a family pet, with no cattle to herd, these little dogs with a big attitude are fiercely protective of their people. They live to serve and will do whatever it takes to please their families.

What a great example for all of us human types, right? That's exactly how we should feel about living for God. We should be excited to work for God and just as enthusiastic to please our heavenly Father. Do you know what pleases Him the most? Following His Holy Commandments and living a life according to the teachings in the Bible. But, in order to know those commandments and teachings, you'll need to read His Word. It's also good to talk to God every day, and we do that through prayer. You don't have to pray formal prayers. Just talk to Him like He is your best friend. That's very pleasing to your heavenly Father.

You know what else pleases God? When He can bless you! He loves you so much and can't wait to show you the plan He has for your life. It's fun to serve God. So, take it from the Welsh Corgi—live to serve and aim to please your Master.

Unleash the Truth: "Therefore, my dear brothers and sisters, stand firm. Let nothing move you. Always give yourselves fully to the work of the Lord, because you know that your labor in the Lord is not in vain." (1 Corinthians 15:58)

Digging Deeper: Do you take time to read the Bible every day? If you don't know where to start, it's good to begin reading one chapter of Psalms and one chapter of Proverbs in the Old Testament. Also, it's great to read in the Gospels—Matthew, Mark, Luke, and John—in the New Testament.

Fido 411: Did you know that the world's most famous Pembroke Welsh Corgi fan was Queen Elizabeth II? She had one or more Corgis at all times from 1933 until her death in 2022.

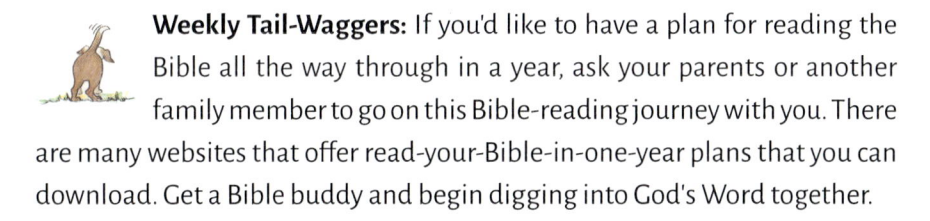

Weekly Tail-Waggers: If you'd like to have a plan for reading the Bible all the way through in a year, ask your parents or another family member to go on this Bible-reading journey with you. There are many websites that offer read-your-Bible-in-one-year plans that you can download. Get a Bible buddy and begin digging into God's Word together.

Michelle

Pomeranian

Group: Toy

Size: 6 to 7 inches; 3 to 7 pounds

Origin: This breed's name comes from Pomerania, a region now located in Germany and Poland. It is part of the Spitz family of sledding dogs. It started out larger and mostly white in color, but through the years, it has become much smaller in size.[1] Queen Victoria brought Poms from Italy in 1888 and started breeding them, causing their popularity to rise. By the 1900s, they were being shown in England and America in a variety of colors.

This adored breed has won Best in Show at Westminster only once, in 1988.

AKC: 1888

Big Faith

Poms are a hit wherever they go. They are cute, alert, intelligent, easy to train, and fun to be around. (Yes, they have been known to do tricks and be "the class clown" from time to time.) Poms are the perfect companion and the tiniest watchdog you'll ever love. With its double coat, it appears like a fantastic little fluff ball, but don't call your Pom little. You see, Poms have been nicknamed "the little dog who thinks he can" because these dainty dogs come with big attitudes.

This bigger-than-life confidence can be both a blessing and a curse for this breed. While a Pom can command a room and entertain its family for hours, it also won't back down from a fight—even if that fight is with a much larger dog. This breed has even been known to *pick* a fight with a larger animal. Some owners of Poms make their dogs wear a special harness with a handle on top when going out for a walk. Why? So the owner can quickly pick up a Pom who decides to provoke a bigger dog.

While we may not wear an actual harness with a handle on our backs for God to quickly remove us from danger, He still comes through, right on time, every single time. When we become overconfident and take on a problem way too big for us, isn't it nice to know that God has our backs? It's OK to have a big attitude, as long as you have big faith and rely on our big God. Take a note from the Pom, walk in confidence with an attitude of "I think I can."

Unleash the Truth: "But the Lord is faithful, and he will strengthen you and protect you from the evil one." (2 Thessalonians 3:3)

Digging Deeper: Do you struggle with pride? Have you ever tried to solve a problem without asking for help because you thought you could handle it? How did that turn out?

Fido 411: Did you know some pretty distinguished folks in history loved and owned Poms including Michelangelo, Isaac Newton, and Wolfgang Amadeus Mozart?[2]

Weekly Tail-Waggers: Grab your journal and write down what you think having Big Faith means. Now, think of some ways you can show your Big Faith this week. For example, maybe you could step outside your comfort zone and volunteer to lead a Bible club at your school or in your neighborhood?

Michelle

Poodle

GROUP Non-sporting

SIZE *standard*—more than 15 inches tall; 40 to 70 pounds, *miniature*—10 to 15 inches tall; 10 to 15 pounds, *toy*—10 inches and under; 4 to 6 pounds

ORIGIN Although it's known as the national dog of France, some believe poodles actually came from Germany.1

A standard poodle won Best in Show at Westminster in 1935, 1958, 1973, and 1991. A miniature won in 1943, 1959, and 2002. A toy won in 1956 and 1961.

AKC 1887

Don't Judge a Dog by Its Fur

Poodles are often seen as fussy, little diva-like dogs who are more beauty than brains. You might've thought that, too, because of the way many poodles are groomed. With puffs of hair tied on top of their head, they look like little prissy pooches, don't they? (I've even seen a toy poodle whose fur was dyed pink!)

But you shouldn't judge a dog by its fur. According to the American Kennel Club, the poodle is one of the smartest dog breeds around. In fact, some experts say there is only one breed smarter than poodles—Border Collies.

Poodles are known to be not only fast learners but also great athletes. Ever watched dogs compete for agility titles? They sprint through an obstacle course, running through tubes and leaping over bars. It's crazy! Poodles rule in agility competitions.

So, you might say, poodles are stunning, smart, and strong. They are so much more than their prissy puffs of fur tied with pretty pink bows. You have to look past all of that to really get to know this impressive breed.

You know, poodles aren't the only ones who are misjudged at times. We humans do it all the time. Maybe you've been quick to judge others by what they look like or how they dress, or maybe you've been the one being judged. Either way, it's no fun and it's not fair. We need to see others as God sees them. The Bible says that God looks on a man's heart while everybody else looks on the outward appearance. In other words, God looks past all of the outer stuff and fluff and judges us by who we are on the inside. Isn't that good news?

So, even if you're not a great athlete like the poodle, and even if you're not the prettiest girl or the handsomest guy in your class, it doesn't matter to God. He loves the *you* that He sees—the kind, clever, funny, unique person that you are. He made you and He thinks you're the top dog!

Unleash the Truth: "For you formed my inward parts; you knitted me together in my mother's womb. I praise you, for I am fearfully and wonderfully made." (Psalm 139:13-14 ESV)

Digging Deeper: How does it make you feel to know that the Creator of the Universe also created you? And He took His time to make you just right!

Fido 411: Did you know the English word *poodle* comes from the German word *pudel*, which means to splash in the water? Poodles are great swimmers, according to the American Kennel Club.[2]

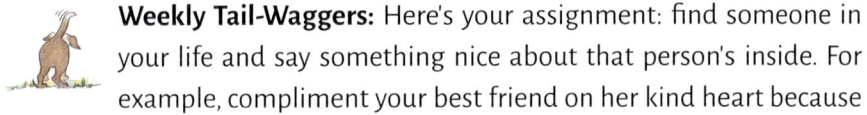

Weekly Tail-Waggers: Here's your assignment: find someone in your life and say something nice about that person's inside. For example, compliment your best friend on her kind heart because she is always so sweet to everybody—even when they aren't sweet to her. Find a different person to compliment each day this week.

Michelle

Pug

Group Toy

Size 10 to 13 inches; 14 to 18 pounds

Origin Pugs originated in China more than two thousand years ago. They were prized possessions of the emperors of China.[1]

A Pug took Best in Show at Westminster in 1981. It was the first Best in Show win for the Pug breed. They have also taken Best in Group nine times.[2]

AKC 1885

The Pug Life

According to the American Kennel Club, the Pug is just about the perfect dog. A book of breed standards describes them as even-tempered, stable, playful, charming, dignified, outgoing, loving, and extremely adaptable. They even go so far as to say, "No other dog can equal the Pug in his virtues as a family pet."[3] That's their way of saying a Pug is an all-around good egg, uh, dog.

Basically, a Pug can get along with pretty much anybody. He loves kids and other dogs. And he wants to do whatever his owner wants to do. Really, all he wants is to love his people and be loved by them. Simple joys.

Getting along with just about everybody is a Pug trait we should all have. People who stir up trouble or are hard to get along with are *not* good representatives of God's kingdom. The Bible tells us that we should live in peace with everyone if we possibly can. There are situations and circumstances where it might not be possible. We can't control what other people do, but we *can* control what *we* do. As followers of Jesus Christ, we always want to make sure that we represent Him well. And you can be sure that people notice.

So what's the secret to getting along with everyone? A Pug's life gives us a pretty good idea. Keep your cool. Be dependable and playful and charming. Be the first one to say hello and introduce yourself. Keep a sense of humor, and be ready to roll with the punches. And above all, love others. By this everyone will know that you belong to the King of Kings.

Unleash the Truth: "If it is possible, as far as it depends on you, live at peace with everyone." (Romans 12:18)

"A new command I give you: Love one another. As I have loved you, so you must love one another. By this everyone will know that you are my disciples, if you love one another." (John 13:34–35)

Digging Deeper: What are some ways you can get along with others?

Fido 411: The folds on a Pugs face give them a sad look, but Pugs are really cheerful dogs with outgoing personalities. However, it is important to keep those folds clean to prevent infection caused by food, water, and other small bits of debris that sometimes get trapped there.[4]

Weekly Tail-Waggers: Think about how well you get along with others. Is there someone you have trouble with? Pray about how you can get along with this person better. Ask the Lord to show you what you can do to improve your relationship.

Wendy

Puggle

GROUP — Crossbreed

SIZE — 13 to 15 inches; 18 to 30 pounds[1]

ORIGIN — A Puggle is a "designer dog" created by crossing a Pug and a Beagle. The breed was developed in the United States in the 1990s.[2]

Like other crossbreeds, Puggles do not compete in American Kennel Club events. However, they are great companion dogs and often excel at agility contests.[3]

AKC — The Puggle is not recognized by the AKC.

Push Away from the Table!

Puggles are sweet-natured dogs with many wonderful qualities. They're great family dogs, and they get along well with strangers and other dogs. It's no wonder they have become one of the most popular dogs in America.

Puggles also have one not-so-great trait they inherit from both Pugs and Beagles. They really, really like to eat. In fact, they like it so much they often don't know when to quit. Puggles will eat until they are about ready to pop! If a Puggle owner isn't careful, their sweet little dog can turn into a pudgy Puggle in a hurry. And, just as with people, an overweight dog usually has more than their share of health issues.

Overeating is a problem—whether it's a dog or a person. The Bible calls it gluttony. Gluttony is often listed as one of the seven greatest sins because it not only leads to health problems but also is a sign that a person is no longer putting God first in their lives. In a way, food can become a person's idol, that is, something that takes God's place. Because food is something we *need* in order to live, people are sometimes unaware that they are actually living to eat.

Our goal in life should be to put God first—in every area of our lives. Where our bodies are concerned, we must remember that we are the temple of the Holy Spirit. Someday, when we go to heaven, we'll have a new body that never gets sick or breaks down. Until then it's our job to take care of the body we have as a way to honor God. And controlling our appetite is one way we do that.

Unleash the Truth: "Do not join those who drink too much wine or gorge themselves on meat, for drunkards and gluttons become poor, and drowsiness clothes them in rags." (Proverbs 23:20–21)

"For the kingdom of God is not a matter of eating and drinking, but of righteousness, peace and joy in the Holy Spirit." (Romans 14:17)

"Do you not know that your bodies are temples of the Holy Spirit, who is in you, whom you have received from God? You are not your own; you were bought at a price. Therefore honor God with your bodies." (1 Corinthians 6:19–20)

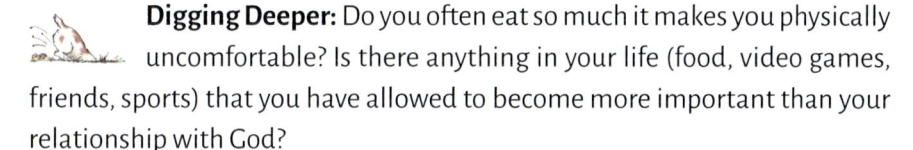

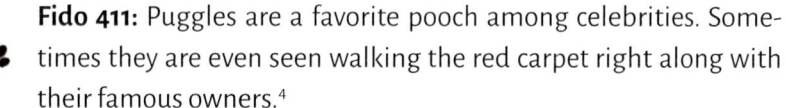

Digging Deeper: Do you often eat so much it makes you physically uncomfortable? Is there anything in your life (food, video games, friends, sports) that you have allowed to become more important than your relationship with God?

Fido 411: Puggles are a favorite pooch among celebrities. Sometimes they are even seen walking the red carpet right along with their famous owners.[4]

Weekly Tail-Waggers: Spend some time this week examining your favorite things. Consider whether any of those things have taken God's place in your heart. If you find something has become an "idol" in your life, ask God to forgive you and show you how to get rid of it.

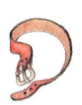

Wendy

Puli

GROUP   Herding

SIZE   16 to 17 inches; 25 to 35 pounds

ORIGIN   The Puli arrived in Europe with Asian nomads who used them for sheep herding in the Hungarian plains. Their unique coats are soft and wooly underneath with long thick outer cords. They still have a compelling tendency to be herders.

The Puli has never won Best in Show at Westminster but did take top honors at the AKC National Championship in 2016.

AKC   The AKC recognized the breed in 1936, only a year after they came to America.

You're Covered!

Pulik (plural for Puli) are beautiful, unusual-looking dogs with their wooly coats that hang in dreadlocks all over their bodies. But, under all of that fur, you'll find a strong and active dog who is quite light on its feet. Because it's hard to tell if this dog is coming or going, it's been nicknamed "push-me, pull-me." A Puli's coat can be black, white, or gray, and despite its corded, heavy coat, this dog doesn't shed! So, it's considered hypoallergenic.

    The Puli's coat is not only beautiful but it's also very functional. It is dense and weatherproof. That's right, this dog's corded coat is able to protect the Puli from extremely cold weather while herding sheep on the ranch. In other words, its coat provides a very necessary protective covering.

    We all need a little protective covering once in a while, which is why it's so comforting to know that our heavenly Father provides that for us. According to the Scriptures, God covers and shields us from things that might hurt us. It's almost like He provides a supernatural force field around us. Psalm 3:3–5 says: "But you, O Lord, are a shield around me; you are my glory, the one who holds my head high. I cried out to the Lord, and he answered me from his holy mountain. I lay down and slept, yet I woke up in safety, for the Lord was watching over me" (NLT). God promises to watch over you and provide a shield around you—even better than the Puli's dreadlocks. You can trust God to cover you!

Unleash the Truth: "You are my hiding place! You protect me from trouble, and you put songs in my heart because you have saved me." (Psalm 32:7 CEV)

Digging Deeper: Think of a time when God protected you from danger. Did you take time to thank Him?

Fido 411: Guess what Puli is the wealthiest in America? That would be Beast, a Puli owned by Facebook CEO Mark Zuckerberg.[1]

Weekly Tail-Waggers: Read about a time when God provided protection for one of His servants—a guy named Daniel. (Daniel 6:16–22)

Michelle

Rat Terrier

Group: Terrier

Size: 10 to 18 inches; 10 to 25 pounds

Origin: Rat Terriers are an American breed created in the 1800s by immigrant farmers. They are a blend of Fox Terrier and at least six other breeds.[1]

The Rat Terrier's first Westminster Dog Show appearance was in 2014.[2] Although they haven't won any dog show honors as yet, they excel in agility, obedience, and lure coursing.[3]

AKC: 2013

Keep on Looking, Keep on Praying

A Rat Terrier is a small, sturdy dog with a short, smooth coat. Its coloring is a mix of white with a variety of other colors in large patches. This distinctive pattern makes them easy to spot in the field.[4]

Ratties live to hunt rats and other vermin and can successfully hunt above and below ground. Even if their prey isn't visible, a Rat Terrier will not give up. They continue to search until the object of their hunt is flushed out into the open. Their determination to get what they are looking for has made them the dog of choice on farms all over America for many years.

How successful do you think the Rattie would be if they gave up whenever they couldn't easily see their prey? The very reason they are such great hunters is because they don't stop looking until they find what they are looking for. How about you?

When it comes to our prayers, the Bible tells us it's OK to ask and then keep on asking. When Jesus was teaching his disciples how to pray, he gave them these instructions: "Ask and it will be given to you; seek and you will find; knock and the door will be opened to you. For everyone who asks receives; the one who seeks finds; and to the one who knocks, the door will be opened" (Matthew 7:7–8). Another translation says, "keep on looking and you will keep on finding" (TLB).

The Bible also tells us that it's important to pray according to God's will. The way we know His will is to read His Word. When God's Word is in us (when we have it hidden in our hearts), we can ask in confidence, knowing God will hear and answer us. And it's OK to keep asking. Because Jesus said so!

Unleash the Truth: "And so it is with prayer—keep on asking and you will keep on getting; keep on looking and you will keep on finding; knock and the door will be opened." (Luke 11:9 TLB)

"If you remain in me and my words remain in you, ask whatever you wish, and it will be done for you." (John 15:7)

"This is the confidence we have in approaching God: that if we ask anything according to his will, he hears us." (1 John 5:14)

Digging Deeper: What is it you need from God right now? Have you asked about it? Are you seeking the answer?

Fido 411: One hundred years ago, rat catchers mostly worked their dogs on farms and ranches. Today, a new kind of rat catcher is using Rat Terriers and other dogs who hunt vermin in large urban areas like New York City and Washington, D.C.[5]

Weekly Tail-Waggers: This week start a prayer journal. Make a list of the things you are praying about. Study the list and ask yourself, *Are these things God's will?* If the answer is yes, keep praying about those things until you get an answer!

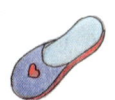

Wendy

Rhodesian Ridgeback
(ro-DEE-zhn)

Group Hound

Size 24 to 27 inches; 70 to 85 pounds

Origin The Rhodesian Ridgeback comes from southern Africa. It gets its name from the ridge of hair that grows along its spine. It is a cross between a domesticated dog from the Khoikhoi tribe and European dogs that came with the Dutch colonists. They were further developed to be big game hunters, which resulted in their nickname of "Lion Dogs." These dogs also had a protective nature that kept other predators away from the hunters. As big game hunting decreased in southern Africa, this breed almost became extinct.

The Rhodesian Ridgeback has never won Best in Show at Westminster.

AKC 1955

What Defines You?

The Rhodesian Ridgeback comes in a variety of colors from light gold to deep auburn. But, that's not what you'll notice first about this magnificent breed. This dog is a large, muscular hound with high set ears, bright eyes, and a ridge of raised fur running down the middle of its back. The Rhodesian Ridgeback might look scary, but it can be a gentle family pet if trained early. However, this breed can turn from sweet to aggressive in a minute if it feels threatened. The Rhodesian Ridgeback will do whatever it takes to keep its owners safe. Of course, there are other breeds who have that same protective instinct.

But the ridge running down the middle of the Rhodesian Ridgeback's spine is one feature that distinguishes it from all other breeds. When you see it, you can tell immediately that dog is a Rhodesian Ridgeback. You know, as Christians we have a telltale feature too. It's called love. The Bible says in John 13:35 that the world will know we are Christians by our love. When someone says something ugly to us, we are to respond in love. Your Christian response—love—will cause others to wonder what makes you different. Your love will draw people to God. It's called being a witness. Like the Rhodesian Ridgeback's line of raised fur down its spine, your Christian love will get the attention of others.

Unleash the Truth: "Make your light shine, so that others will see the good that you do and will praise your Father in heaven." (Matthew 5:16 CEV)

Digging Deeper: It's important that we respond in love, not react in anger when people are mean. Do you walk in love? Do you let your light shine?

Fido 411: Did you know why the Rhodesian Ridgeback's fur running along its spine stands up? Because that fur actually grows in the opposite direction from the dog's all-over fur.

Weekly Tail-Waggers: The next time someone acts ugly to you, take a minute, and breathe so that you can respond in love and not react in anger. Practice walking in love every single day.

Michelle

Rottweiler

Group: Working

Size: 22 to 27 inches; 80 to 135 pounds

Origin: The Rottweiler's ancestors were Roman army dogs used to guard the herds of animals that they brought with them for food. After the collapse of the Roman Empire, the dogs were used in the cattle town of Rottweil, Germany, moving cattle to market. In the 1800s, railroads began moving cattle, so Rottweilers were then used as police dogs and guard dogs. They also served as some of the first guide dogs for the blind. Today, they are often used as search-and-rescue dogs when tragedy strikes.

The Rottweiler has never won Best in Show at Westminster or taken the National Championship at the American Kennel Club.

AKC: 1931

Wait and See

Rottweilers are loving and loyal, making them wonderful family dogs! But they can also be very aggressive toward strangers if they feel they need to protect their families. Rottweilers instinctively use a wait-and-see method when they meet new people. If the Rottie's owner is friendly with a new person, then the Rottie will generally accept the stranger. But if the owner doesn't seem comfortable with a new person, the Rottie will not hesitate to protect its human family.

A Rottweiler trusts its owner's instincts and follows suit. In the same way a Rottie watches its master to know how to respond, we should serve Christ with a wait-and-see attitude. It should become an instinct for us to wait for our Master's cue about how to proceed in any situation. We need to wholeheartedly trust His decisions and await His guidance.

When a situation arises, especially one that seems confusing or upsetting, look to Jesus. Pray about what your next action should be, and look in the Bible to see what Jesus might do in the situation you're facing. When you look to Jesus for your answer, you can know that you are getting advice from the wisest source. He not only has all of the answers, He is the Answer! We're so blessed to have the world's best Teacher!

Unleash the Truth: "In all your ways acknowledge him, and he will make straight your paths." (Proverbs 3:6 ESV)

Digging Deeper: Are you facing a situation today that has you feeling uneasy about what to do? Just turn to Jesus and trust His leading.

Fido 411: Even though Rottweilers are big dogs, they often consider themselves lap dogs and lay across their owners' laps![1] Now, that's a big lapdog!

Weekly Tail-Waggers: Take a few minutes today and memorize this Bible verse found in Psalm 119:133: "Guide my steps by your word, so I will not be overcome by evil." (NLT)

Michelle

Russian (Russkiy) Toy
(ROO-skee)

GROUP — Toy

SIZE — 8 to 11 inches; 3 to 6 pounds

ORIGIN — Descended from English Toy Terriers brought to Russia in the 1700s, Russian Toys were popular with the Russian ruling class. About the size of a Chihuahua, they are among the smallest dogs in the world.[1]

The Russian Toy is new to Westminster with its first appearance there in 2022. No awards yet, but it's one to watch in the future.

AKC — 2022

He's Written Your Name on His Hand

After the Communist takeover of Russia, small dogs like the Russian Toy were considered unnecessary. Under Communist rule, only dogs suitable for the military could be bred. It's very likely the little dogs had to be hidden to avoid being destroyed. The Russian Toy, so popular with the old Russian aristocracy, nearly disappeared. It seemed they were forgotten. Even after the Soviet Union fell apart in the 1980s, their numbers continued to decline because of all the Western breeds making their way into the region. In spite of this, there were people who loved the Russian Toy. They did not forget. Due to their efforts, the breed was officially recognized by Russia in 1988. The Russian Toy is still rare but is becoming more popular all the time.[2]

The nation of Israel has gone through hard times too. During the Holocaust of the last century, they had to hide to keep from being destroyed, just like the Russian Toy. And, like the Russian Toy, many of them were destroyed. Today, they face invasion from all sides. I'm sure they wonder if God has forgotten them. But God's Word says He will never forget them. He has written their names on His hand. They are always there in front of Him as a reminder.

Sometimes when Christians go through difficult times, we feel that God has abandoned us—that we are forgotten. It's important to remember that just because we experience hard times, it doesn't mean that God doesn't love us. He sees us. He has written our names on His hand, too, because we have been made a part of His family (the Jews) by adoption. No matter what happens to us in this life, we are His and He is ours. Nothing can change that. And even if we feel unseen or forgotten, we must remember His words: I will not forget you.

Unleash the Truth: "Can a woman forget her nursing child? Can she have no pity on the son to whom she gave birth? Even these may forget, but I will not forget you. See, I have marked your names on My hands. Your walls are always before Me." (Isaiah 49:15–16 NLV)

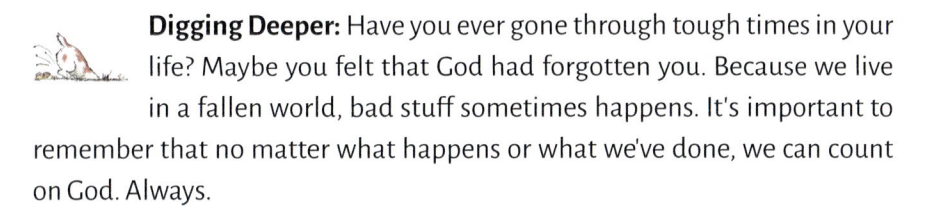

Digging Deeper: Have you ever gone through tough times in your life? Maybe you felt that God had forgotten you. Because we live in a fallen world, bad stuff sometimes happens. It's important to remember that no matter what happens or what we've done, we can count on God. Always.

Fido 411: There are two varieties of Russian Toy—longhaired and smooth coat. The longhaired was thought to have disappeared forever until a longhaired puppy was born to smooth coated parents in Moscow in 1958. This male puppy became the foundation for today's longhaired Russian Toys.[3]

Weekly Tail-Waggers: Take a moment to thank God for always remembering you. Pray this way: "Thank you, God, for loving me and keeping me on Your mind. I don't always feel seen or loved, but I choose to believe that I am. I am Yours and You are mine forever and always. Amen."

Wendy

Saint Bernard

GROUP Working

SIZE 26 to 30 inches; 120 to 180 pounds

ORIGIN The Saint Bernard was originally known as the Talhund and dates back to the late 1600s. The breed was developed by monks of St. Bernard's hospice in the Swiss Alps.[1]

Although the Saint Bernard has participated in the Westminster Dog Show since 1877, it has never taken a Best in Show award.[2]

AKC 1885

Savior to the Rescue

Saint Bernards are no longer used as search-and-rescue dogs, but for about two hundred years they lived and worked in the area of Saint Bernard's monastery in the Swiss Alps. During that time the dogs rescued more than two thousand people.[3]

The monks took their Saint Bernards on all treks outside the monastery because the dogs had a good sense of direction and the ability to find a path even in dense fog or snowstorms. They could sense an avalanche before it occurred. And they could even be sent out in small packs of two or three to hunt for lost travelers without any help from the monks. The people who were lost or stranded in the storms had no way to help themselves. If it weren't for the Saint Bernards, they would have died there.[4]

You know, in many ways, we're like those lost travelers. The Bible says that we *all*, like sheep (or wayward travelers), have gone astray. We're all sinners, and we're all lost—and there's *nothing* we can do to help ourselves. The

Paws-itive Inspirations

only one who can rescue us from our sinful situation is Jesus. But because Jesus gave His life on the cross to pay for our sins, we can be rescued from certain death. When we accept Jesus Christ as Lord and Savior, the penalty for our sin is paid in full, and we are saved! What an awesome thing it is to know we've been rescued by Him!

Unleash the Truth: "We all, like sheep, have gone astray, each of us has turned to our own way." (Isaiah 53:6)

"The Lord will rescue his servants; no one who takes refuge in him will be condemned." (Psalm 34:22)

Digging Deeper: Have you ever had to be rescued? What did you naturally want to do for the person who rescued you? (Hopefully, you wanted to thank them.)

Fido 411: The most famous Saint Bernard was a dog named Barry who lived in the Saint Bernard hospice from about 1800 to 1814. He rescued more than forty people. Since then, the monks at Saint Bernard's hospice always name one of their dogs Barry in his honor.[5]

Weekly Tail-Waggers: Think about how Jesus has rescued you. Because He took your punishment, you can have eternal life with Him.

If you've never asked Jesus to save you, now's the time to do it. You can do this by praying:

Dear Jesus, thank You for taking the punishment for my sins. Please save me, and be the Lord of my life. Forgive me of my sins. Help me to know You and live the rest of my life for You. Amen.

Wendy

151

Samoyed

(suh-MOY-ud) or (sam-uh-YED)

GROUP Working

SIZE 19 to 23.5 inches; 35 to 66 pounds

ORIGIN The Samoyed is one of the most ancient breeds—going back more than five thousand years. It was developed by the nomadic people of the Russian tundra to herd and guard reindeer.[1]

Samoyeds have never won Best in Show at Westminster,[2] but they have placed in their Working group eleven times. They are multi-purpose dogs that also do well in agility, obedience, weight pull, herding, and other performance competitions.[3]

AKC 1906

Staying Out of Trouble

Samoyeds are beautiful white, fluffy dogs. They are friendly and easygoing with an expression that makes them look as though they're always smiling. They have natural herding and guarding instincts and make great sled dogs too.[4]

To a Samoyed, its people are family—and they like hanging out with the family. They also like having plenty of activities to occupy their minds and bodies. A Samoyed who is bored or lonely is very likely to get into trouble. They may dig holes in your landscaping or destroy the cushions on the couch. A happy Samoyed is one who has plenty of physical and mental exercise.[5]

Guess what. People are like that too. When we get bored and have too much time on our hands, we can get into trouble. Of course, this is more true of some people than others, but we all struggle with this from time to time.

Most of us are our best selves when we are physically and mentally active. When we're not, we are more easily tempted to do things we shouldn't.

Think about it. Sitting around and doing nothing usually leads to watching that video you really shouldn't be watching or playing that game your mom told you not to play. It can mean letting our minds go places we shouldn't and thinking about stuff we know isn't good. Rest is good for us, but idleness (doing nothing when we should be doing something) is never a good idea.

Instead, we need to stay focused on doing the work God has given us to do (school or job, good deeds, being kind) and keeping our hearts and minds set on Him. When we are busy doing good things and thinking right thoughts, we can expect blessing and favor from God. And who doesn't want blessing and favor?

Unleash the Truth: "Lazy hands make for poverty, but diligent hands bring wealth." (Proverbs 10:4)

"Set your minds on things above, not on earthly things." (Colossians 3:2)

Digging Deeper: What do you do when you're bored? Has it gotten you in trouble?

Fido 411: For the nomadic peoples of the Russian Tundra, Samoyeds are like family. The dogs have the run of the family tents and often sleep with the children to keep them warm.[6]

Weekly Tail-Waggers: Think about times you have gotten in trouble in the past. Were you restless and bored before that happened? Did being restless and bored lead you to do something you wouldn't ordinarily do? This week think about some things you can do that will use your mind and physical energy in a positive way—one that will glorify God and keep you out of trouble.

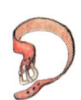

Wendy

Schipperke

(SKIP-er-kee)

GROUP — Non-Sporting

SIZE — 10 to 13 inches; 10 to 16 pounds

ORIGIN — The Schipperke goes back to the 1600s in the Flemish provinces of what is now Belgium. They were originally bred as mascots for skilled labor associations, watchdogs and companions on barges, rat catchers, and herding dogs. Today, they are often used in search and rescue.[1]

A Schipperke took Best in Group in the 2019 Westminster Dog Show. The breed regularly places in that group.[2] They also excel in a variety of other AKC events including obedience, agility, and rally.[3]

AKC — 1904

Training to Reign

Schipperkes are small, black dogs with a foxlike face. They are active watchdogs and rat hunters with playful personalities. And they're smart. Really smart. Put all those smarts with an independent nature, and you're looking at a dog who needs training from an early age. Schipperkes that are properly trained grow up to be wonderful family pets. But a Schipperke that isn't well-trained is miserable and can make everyone around them miserable as well.[4]

The truth is that people need training too. From the time we are babies we have to be taught how to do things. We have to be taught right from wrong. We have to be trained to act properly. If we're not, we can grow up to be hard to get along with or worse. Many people who don't get proper training as a child wind up in prison because they don't follow the rules of society.

Christians need training too. Just because we accept Jesus Christ as our Savior doesn't mean we automatically know how to *be* a Christian. Our training includes prayer, praise and worship, Bible study, and meeting with other believers. When we do these things, we "grow in Christ." We become more mature believers. The best part is, all the training we get by doing these things isn't just for the life we live now. The Bible tells us we are also being trained to rule and reign with Him someday. That's pretty exciting. We're in training for the life we have now—*and* for the one we will have in heaven someday.

Unleash the Truth: "Everyone who competes in the games goes into strict training. They do it to get a crown that will not last, but we do it to get a crown that will last forever." (1 Corinthians 9:25)

"Have nothing to do with godless myths and old wives' tales; rather, train yourself to be godly." (1 Timothy 4:7)

Digging Deeper: What activities do you currently participate in that are part of your Christian training?

Fido 411: Schipperkes are best known as barge dogs on the canals of Belgium. The name *Schipperke* means "little boatman," although they are often affectionately called Belgium's "Little Captain."[5]

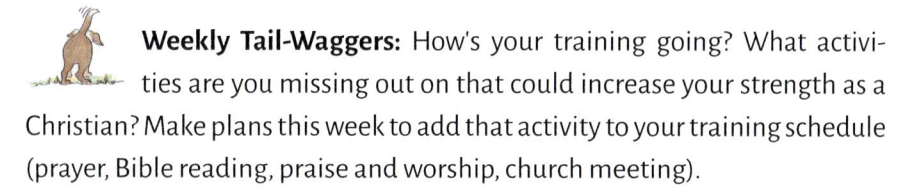

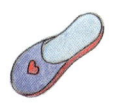

Weekly Tail-Waggers: How's your training going? What activities are you missing out on that could increase your strength as a Christian? Make plans this week to add that activity to your training schedule (prayer, Bible reading, praise and worship, church meeting).

Wendy

Scottish Deerhound

GROUP Hound

SIZE 28 to 32 inches; 70 to 130 pounds

ORIGIN Scottish Deerhounds are shaggier versions of their cousins, the Irish wolfhounds. People often confuse the two. Dating back as far as the sixteenth century, Scottish Deerhounds were bred to help the wealthy hunt deer.[1] They love to run, and they actually need to run every day.

A female Scottish Deerhound named Hickory won Best in Show at the 2011 Westminster Dog Show, making her the first of her breed to win that title.[2]

AKC 1886

Faith for Everyone

As early as the sixteenth century, the Scottish Deerhound developed a fan following. It was a favorite of Scottish royalty. In fact, the breed was so highly favored that anyone who ranked lower than an earl could not own a Scottish Deerhound. So if you lived back in the sixteenth century and fell in love with that breed and wanted more than anything to own one but weren't a royal, you were just simply out of luck.

Unfortunately, throughout history there are lots of examples of this kind of hierarchy and unfair treatment of those who didn't "measure up" for whatever reason—class, color of skin, educational or economical status, and more. But you know where you're always accepted, qualified, and loved? In God's family. Yep, you're a child of God, and you didn't have to earn that status. And here's what else—no one can take it away from you. I find it so comforting that God loves us no matter what, and He loves us all exactly the same! We all get to be His favorite child—how awesome is that?

Oh, and here's more good news. You no longer have to be royalty to own a Scottish Deerhound. Yay!

Unleash the Truth: "I have loved you with an everlasting love; I have drawn you with unfailing kindness." (Jeremiah 31:3)

Digging Deeper: Have you ever been excluded from a club or treated unfairly for no good reason? How did that make you feel? If this ever happens again, just remember that you are loved by the Creator of the Universe. You are special. You matter.

Fido 411: Sir Walter Scott was a big fan of Scottish Deerhounds. He not only owned one but also featured a Scottish Deerhound in his novel *The Talisman*.[3]

Weekly Tail-Waggers: The next time you see someone sitting alone, why not be a friend and sit next to that person? Or if you notice someone being left out, try to include that person.

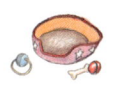

Michelle

Scottish Terrier

GROUP Terrier

SIZE 10 inches; 18 to 22 pounds

ORIGIN Simply put, Scotties are from Scotland but there is more to the story. Apparently, early on, all terrier-type dogs from Scotland were referred to as "Scottish terriers" when they weren't actually Scottish Terriers at all. To make matters even more confusing, today's Scottish Terriers were once grouped with Skye Terriers. At any rate, Scotties are from Scotland, and they didn't make their way to the United States until 1883.[1]

Scotties have taken top honors at the Westminster Kennel Club eight times since 1911, with the breed's most recent win in 2010.[2]

AKC 1885

Be a Diehard for God!

Scotties are adorable short-legged dogs that are probably best known for their bushy eyebrows and beard. They come in many coat colors but are more commonly seen with black fur when featured on home decor and fashion items. Because they are so cute and distinctive, they have made their way into the homes and hearts of many.

Scottish Terriers were originally bred to be brave hunters, and that instinct runs deep in their souls. In fact, these little determined dogs made a name for themselves under the leadership of military man George the Fourth, Earl of Dumbarton. He ruled over a pack of Scotties who proved so courageous in battle that they were nicknamed "The diehards." People knew about them all over Scotland!

Paws-itive Inspirations

Wouldn't it be wonderful if people looked at our bravery and determination to serve Jesus and said, "Now, that's a diehard Christian!" That's called being a witness for God. When we serve Him with all of our heart, people will notice. When you stand up for the girl who is being bullied in the lunchroom, people will notice your kindness and bravery. When you treat your parents with respect and show them honor by doing your chores the first time you're asked, others will notice. Keep serving Jesus with your whole heart and pretty soon, you may be called a diehard—a diehard Christian!

Unleash the Truth: "But in your hearts honor Christ the Lord as holy, always being prepared to make a defense to anyone who asks you for a reason for the hope that is in you; yet do it with gentleness and respect." (1 Peter 3:15 ESV)

Digging Deeper: Being a witness can work both positively and negatively. In other words, you can be a good witness for God or a bad witness for God. Which are you?

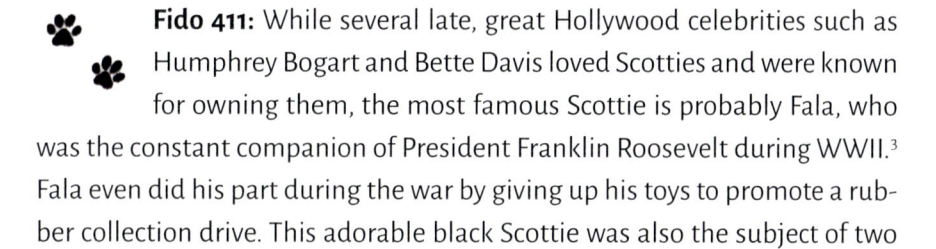

Fido 411: While several late, great Hollywood celebrities such as Humphrey Bogart and Bette Davis loved Scotties and were known for owning them, the most famous Scottie is probably Fala, who was the constant companion of President Franklin Roosevelt during WWII.[3] Fala even did his part during the war by giving up his toys to promote a rubber collection drive. This adorable black Scottie was also the subject of two MGM films![4]

Weekly Tail-Waggers: Do you have a nickname? If someone were to give you a nickname based on your attitude, what would it be?

Michelle

Shetland Sheepdog (Shelties)

GROUP Herding

SIZE 13 to 16 inches; 15 to 25 pounds

ORIGIN The Shelties are a smaller version of the Collie from the Shetland Islands, the northernmost point of the United Kingdom. They were used on farms to herd sheep, ponies, and poultry. They were called toonie dogs (*toon* being the Shetland word for farm). They lived in these remote islands away from other breeds until the early twentieth century. In 1909 the Kennel Club of England registered this breed as the Shetland Collie but soon changed its name to Shetland Sheepdog.

Although Shelties have never won Best in Show at Westminster or in the AKC National Championship, they are known as one of the most obedient breeds.

AKC 1911

Hold Your Bark

The Shetland Sheepdog is a small, energetic herding dog that looks a lot like its cousin the Collie. Shelties have lovely long coats and come in black, blue merle, and sable with white markings. While they make great affectionate pets, they also can be a bit standoffish with strangers. And, they are quite the barkers! Of course, being a barker and not too trusting of strangers makes this breed perfect for watchdog duties.

Shelties are a popular breed, but even those who love these amazing little dogs will tell you they are very vocal! In fact, excessive barking is one of the main complaints that Sheltie owners have concerning their beloved pets.

If left alone for too many hours, a Shetland Sheepdog will most assuredly bark—a lot. If there's too much roughhousing going on, a Sheltie will bark. And, if scolded in too harsh of a voice, again, a Sheltie is guaranteed to talk back—and bark a lot. They almost can't help themselves; they are just loud and frequent barkers.[1]

How about you? Have you been known to be too vocal from time to time? Do you talk back when being corrected? Do you talk too much when you're feeling nervous or upset? If so, you might have been a Sheltie if you'd been born a dog. And, you know what? That's OK. God understands because He made you and your mouth! And, He gives each of us the fruit of the Spirit once we become Christians, which guarantees self-control. Galatians 5:22–23 says, "But the fruit of the Spirit is love, joy, peace, forbearance, kindness, goodness, faithfulness, gentleness, and self-control."

When we have self-control, we can stop ourselves from reacting with harsh words. Instead, we will be able to respond with silence or by choosing words that are kind. So, if you struggle with "barking" nonstop or talking back, ask God to put a watch over your mouth so that you can practice self-control.

Unleash the Truth: "Everyone enjoys a fitting reply; it is wonderful to say the right thing at the right time!" (Proverbs 15:23 NLT)

Digging Deeper: Do you have trouble controlling your mouth? Be honest; do you react with harsh words before you can stop yourself?

Fido 411: Did you know Miley Cyrus owns a Sheltie named Emu?

Weekly Tail-Waggers: Here's your challenge this week. Keep track of how often you talk back when you should remain silent or respond in love. Then, pray over each time you messed up and ask God to help you do better.

Michelle

Shih Tzu
(SHEED-zoo)

Group Toy

Size 9 to 10.5 inches; 9 to 16 pounds

Origin Although the Shih Tzu came by way of breeding dogs from Tibet, it is steeped in Chinese history. This breed, also known as "little lion dog," is believed to be a cross between the Lhasa Apso and the Pekingese. They were a favorite of royalty and for many years lived only in palaces. It was not until the 1960s that they became popular in the United States.

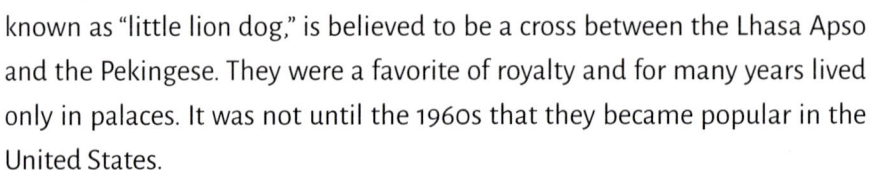

Although the Shih Tzu starred in a movie titled *Best in Show* in 2000, it has never achieved the honor at Westminster.

AKC 1969

We All Need Somebody

This small, confident breed is one of the most beautiful dogs in the world when it is groomed. With its flowing fur that sweeps the ground, a Shih Tzu glides into a room and makes you take notice. While they were originally bred for royal Chinese families and were probably accustomed to sleeping on silk pillows, these little friendly fur balls are not snobby at all! They pretty much love all people and animals—even cats!

   Shih Tzu are very social animals, which can be a problem if they are left alone too often. This breed has been known to experience separation anxiety when its owners are gone for extended periods of time, causing distress in some dogs. For this reason, several dog experts and breeders suggest buying Shih Tzu in pairs! (What could be more fun that two Shih Tzu, right?) Having a pair of Shih Tzu can help boost their mental and physical health and make their lives much happier.[1]

What about you? Do you feel sad when you're alone? Do you experience separation anxiety when you are away from your family and friends? Well, I have good news for you. You're never really alone! The Bible tells us in Hebrews 13:5 that God will never leave us! So, even if you're alone, you're never *really* alone. God is always with you, and here's more good news. He wants to be your friend, your best friend! You can talk to Him just like you talk to your closest buddy—tell Him all of your hopes, dreams, secrets, fears, and everyday stuff too. He loves when you spend time with Him.

Unleash the Truth: "I no longer call you servants, because a servant does not know his master's business. Instead, I have called you friends, for everything that I learned from my Father I have made known to you." (John 15:15)

Digging Deeper: Are you a social person, or are you happiest when you're just with a few friends? How could you stretch yourself to make more friends this week?

Fido 411: The Shih-Tzu is sometimes called the Chrysanthemum dog because its facial hair grows out from its nose, resembling petals.

Weekly Tail-Waggers: Here's your assignment: Make a new friend this week by stepping outside your comfort zone and being friendly. Maybe sit next to that person at school who always eats lunch alone or simply say hello to someone new this week. You have to be a friend to have a friend.

Michelle

Siberian Husky

GROUP Working

SIZE 20 to 23.5 inches; 35 to 60 pounds

ORIGIN The Siberian Husky's ancestors were created by the Chukchi people of northeastern Asia as a sled dog.[1]

The Siberian Husky has taken Best in Show at Westminster one time since 1933 and placed in its Working group fourteen times.[2] They do well in agility, obedience, and tracking competitions and are frequent winners in sled racing.[3]

AKC 1930

Fully Protected

Siberian Huskies are medium-sized dogs with thick, double coats of fur, ears that stand straight up, and bushy tails that keep its face warm when it sleeps. They can travel long distances carrying light loads, and their thick fur coats keep them warm in even the most brutal cold.[4]

The ability to handle the coldest temperatures makes Huskies the perfect dog to pull sleds in the far north. In 1925 a diphtheria (a serious infection of the nose and throat) outbreak in Nome, Alaska, meant a vaccine was needed to prevent an epidemic. The vaccine had to be brought in from Anchorage by sled dog teams. The majority of the trip was led by a Husky named Togo. After a grueling 260 miles, Togo's team handed the vaccine off to another team led by a six-year-old Husky named Balto. Balto and the other dogs battled a fierce blizzard and a treacherous river crossing to get the vaccine to Nome. Balto and his team were hailed as heroes by the entire country for their efforts. There's even a statue of Balto in New York City's Central Park.[4]

Huskies can survive blizzard conditions because of their thick, double coat of fur. It serves as an insulator and prevents freezing water from getting to their skin. In many ways their fur is like a protective armor.

We have armor too. Did you know that? The Bible tells us all about it in Ephesians 6. We have a belt of truth, a breastplate of righteousness, shoes of the gospel, a shield of faith, a helmet of salvation, and a sword of the Spirit. If we are careful to put on this armor daily, we can stand firm as believers no matter what is happening around us. We can be ready for good times and bad.

Being a Christian makes us part of the family of God. It also makes us the enemy of God's enemy: Satan. But we don't have to worry about that because God has given us the armor we need to be fully protected. We just have to make sure to wear it every day.

Unleash the Truth: "Therefore put on the full armor of God, so that when the day of evil comes, you may be able to stand your ground, and after you have done everything, to stand." (Ephesians 6:13)

Digging Deeper: Why would a Christian need to wear armor?

Fido 411: Siberian Huskies have proved their value as superior sled dogs in many polar expeditions. During World War II they were used in the US Army's Arctic Search and Rescue Unit.[5]

Weekly Tail-Waggers: This week be sure to take the time to read Ephesians 6, especially the section on the armor of God in verses 10 through 17. Think about each part of the armor and what it protects. For example: the helmet of salvation protects the mind of the believer. Satan may try to tell you you're not good enough for God, but our salvation means God loved us enough to send His son to die for our sins. Our salvation serves as a helmet to protect our minds.

Wendy

Soft Coated Wheaten Terrier

GROUP — Terrier

SIZE — 17 to 19 inches; 30 to 40 pounds

ORIGIN — Bred in Ireland, the Soft-Coated Wheaten Terrier shares the same roots as the Kerry Blue and Irish Terriers. They were bred to be versatile farm dogs, but they also make the best companion dogs because of their gentle and calm personality.

Although a Wheaten has never won Best in Show at Westminster, one did take Best in Group in 1989. And in 1989, a Wheaten named Andover Song 'N Dance Man was the winner of the Terrier Group.[1]

AKC — 1973

Faith for Everyone

Wheatens have been described as enthusiastic dogs. If you've ever owned one, you know what it's like to enter a room and get a "Wheaten greetin'" with lots of twirls and jumps of happiness. Whether you've been gone five years or five minutes, you'll get the same enthusiastic reaction. They are known for their playful puppylike attitude well into adulthood. They are good-natured, happy dogs who love life and love their families.

We can learn from the Wheaten's cheerful, enthusiastic attitude, especially the way they greet their masters. We should be just as joyful when we greet our Master—our heavenly Father. Just think: every time we pray or read the Bible, we get to enter into the presence of Almighty God. And here's even more good news! He is just as excited to spend time with you!

God loves it when we take time to talk to Him each day and simply spend time thinking about Him and His Word. (That's why it tells us in the Bible in Joshua 1:8 to meditate on His Word day and night.) So go ahead and get excited to spend time with God. You might even do a "Wheaten greetin'"— He would probably love that!

Unleash the Truth: "Never be lazy in your work, but serve the Lord enthusiastically." (Romans 12:11 TLB)

Digging Deeper: Do you have a private time each day with God? It's the best! You don't have to spend hours and hours. Just find ten to fifteen minutes each day and read your Bible and talk to God, just like you'd talk to your best friend.

Fido 411: A Soft Coated Wheaten Terrier named Krista almost made the top 10 in the 2016 national diving dog championship, jumping ten feet two inches into the water. That's super impressive when you consider Krista was up against retrievers, which are actually bred to dive and swim.

Weekly Tail-Waggers: Grab a notebook or your journal and write three reasons you're excited to spend time with God. For example, I would write: I love praying to God because I can tell Him anything!

Michelle

Standard Schnauzer

Group: Working

Size: 17.5 to 19.5 inches; 30 to 50 pounds

Origin: The Schnauzer has been the German's breed of all-purpose farm dog as far back as the Middle Ages. They were used as ratters, herders, guardians, and hunters. They have been in the United States since the 1900s.

The Standard Schnauzer took Best in Show at Westminster in 1997.

AKC: 1904

Be a Quick Learner

The Standard Schnauzer is a medium-sized dog so adorable and smart that early breeders decided to develop two more breeds of different sizes just like it—the Miniature Schnauzer and the Giant Schnauzer.

It's no wonder why breeders wanted to duplicate this dog in different sizes for different needs. Standard Schnauzers are not only highly intelligent and excellent family companions but also very handsome and noble in appearance. They are known for their devotion and protective instincts when it comes to their families. They are almost too smart for their own good. Some have described the Schnauzer as a dog with a human brain. This breed is a very quick learner, and let's face it, that's a very good trait to have whether you are a dog or a human.

Being a quick learner isn't always about learning a new skill; sometimes being a quick learner is about being obedient. The apostle Paul wrote, "Whatever you have learned or received or heard from me, or seen in me—put it into practice. And the God of peace will be with you" (Philippians 4:9). In other words, if you hear your pastor say that God wants you to do unto others as you'd have them do unto you, and then you treat someone badly, you still have some learning and obeying to do. Be a quick learner like the Schnauzer! Don't just hear the Word of God and forget it; be a doer of the Word. And, when you mess up, be quick to say you're sorry and try to do better in the future so that the God of peace will be with you.

Unleash the Truth: "Respect and obey the Lord! This is the beginning of knowledge. Only a fool rejects wisdom and good advice." (Proverbs 1:7 CEV)

Digging Deeper: Are you open to learning new things? When you make a mistake, are you quick to say you're sorry?

Fido 411: Did you know the word *schnauzer* in German has come to mean "whiskered snout"?

Weekly Tail-Waggers: Write down five new skills in your journal that you'd like to learn sometime and begin working on that list this week. It's a good idea to tell a friend or a family member about your quest to learn these new skills so that person can keep you on track and cheer you on.

Michelle

Weimaraner
(VY-mah-rah-ner) or (WY-mah-rah-ner)

GROUP Sporting

SIZE 23 to 27 inches; 55 to 90 pounds

ORIGIN Weimaraners were developed in Germany. Originally bred to hunt big game, they were later used for retrieving birds. Until about 1929, ownership of a Weimaraner was limited to Germany's ruling class.[1]

The Weimaraner has taken first in the Sporting group at Westminster three times since it first competed there in 1943. In addition, "Weims" do well in events such as obedience, agility, rally competitions, and are especially good trackers.[2]

AKC 1943

Nothing Can Separate You from God's Love

Weimaraners are large, active, intelligent dogs that are avid hunters. They require an active owner because they need lots of exercise. They're always happy to join their owners in physical activities like running and swimming. And their beautiful gray coat and amber, gray, or blue-gray eyes have earned them the nickname "Gray Ghost."

But one of the most prominent characteristics of a "Weim" is their strong desire to stay close to their owner. They can and do develop separation anxiety in situations where they are not kept in the house near the family. Their anxiety can be so extreme that it leads to destructive behaviors and lots of loud barking. A Weim who doesn't have his family nearby is one unhappy pup.[3]

The same can be said of Christians. We should desire to stay as close to our heavenly Father as possible. When we try to live for Him daily and talk with Him (pray), we experience the peace that can only come from a close relationship with Him. When we allow activities or other interests to interfere with our relationship, we soon find ourselves feeling lost, unhappy, and maybe even involved in some destructive behavior of our own. The best way to make sure that doesn't happen is to maintain our relationship with God through frequent prayer, daily Bible reading, and fellowship with other believers. There might be days when you don't feel especially close to God, but always remember: there is nothing that can separate you from the love of God. How do I know? The Bible says so!

Unleash the Truth: "No power in the sky above or in the earth below—indeed, nothing in all creation will ever be able to separate us from the love of God that is revealed in Christ Jesus our Lord." (Romans 8:39 NLT)

Digging Deeper: Take some time to think about your day-to-day relationship with God. Is prayer something you only do when things aren't going well? Do you only turn to God in emergencies? Or is God truly your friend?

Fido 411: In the 1970s a photographer named William Wegman began using his Weimaraners in his photo and video work. His photos of Weims posing in odd settings and elaborate costumes became famous all over the world.[4]

Weekly Tail-Waggers: After thinking about your current relationship with God, set some goals for yourself that will help you get closer to Him. You might set aside some time each day to read your Bible. You could spend some time listening to praise music and singing to God. The best way to be closer to God is to spend more time with Him.

Wendy

Welsh Terrier

GROUP — Terrier

SIZE — 15 inches; 20 pounds; females are a bit smaller

ORIGIN — The Welsh Terrier's origin is not really known but was becoming the breed we know by the 1700s. The dog was bred to be a hunter of foxes, otters, and badgers in the mountain regions of Wales.

The Welsh Terrier last won Best in Show at Westminster in 1944.

AKC — 1888

Calm, Cool, and Collected

Welsh Terriers are adorable medium-sized dogs with a close-to-the-body wire-haired coat. Though Welsh Terrier puppies are usually born almost all black, they will eventually develop into black and tan. That's the only color combination of this breed. Like most terriers, Welshies are alert and spirited pups, but compared to other terrier dogs, Welsh Terriers are far calmer and less quarrelsome. In other words, they are more easygoing than most dogs. While other dogs might become jealous when they don't get the attention they crave, Welsh Terriers are not prone to getting jealous or acting out when their owners aren't paying enough attention to them.[1]

These friendly dogs can be a great model for how we should live as Christians. We have no reason to be jealous of others because we know that there are enough blessings and love to go around. Our heavenly Father has more than enough to give! Instead of arguing, stressing out, or being jealous when we don't get exactly what we want, we can patiently wait and continue praying. We don't have to be jealous when a friend succeeds; instead, we can celebrate with that friend. Why? Because we know that God has success in store for us too!

Our best example of how to live is Jesus. When we read about Jesus in the Bible, we can see that He was slow to anger; He didn't pick fights; and He didn't lash out, even when others attacked Him. We should try to live the same way! Like the Welsh Terrier, do your best to be easygoing and pleasant—no matter what. And, remember this classic acronym: WWJD—What Would Jesus Do?

Unleash the Truth: "Therefore be imitators of God, as beloved children. And walk in love, as Christ loved us and gave himself up for us, a fragrant offering and sacrifice to God." (Ephesians 5:1-2 ESV)

Digging Deeper: How did you react the last time things didn't go the way you wanted? Was that the best way to respond? Do you ever feel jealous? How do you handle those feelings?

Fido 411: Welsh Terriers have made it to the White House! The daughter of President John F. Kennedy, Caroline Kennedy, had a Welsh Terrier named Charlie.[2]

Weekly Tail-Waggers: Today, thank God for everything He has given you. Create a list of things that you are grateful for before presenting Him with your requests. When you count your blessings, it's much harder to focus on petty jealousies and disappointments.

Michelle

West Highland White Terrier

GROUP Terrier

SIZE 10 to 11 inches; 15 to 20 pounds

ORIGIN West Highland White Terriers were developed in Scotland to hunt foxes, otters, badgers, and rodents. Credit for the breed goes to Colonel Edward Malcolm. He became determined to develop a white dog after he accidently shot one of his favorite reddish-brown dogs because he mistook it for a fox.[1]

The West Highland White Terrier has taken top honors at Westminster two times since its first entry in 1906. However, its last title was more than sixty years ago.[2]

AKC 1908

Watch Out for the Big Head

West Highland White Terriers, or Westies as they are often called, are smart little dogs that are strong and agile. They're great trackers with enough spunk and courage to take on a fox. And they're known for having a cheerful personality.

On top of all that, Westies have tons of self-confidence. So much so that they can get kind of full of themselves. Sometimes we call that "getting the big head." They can become bossy with other dogs if they haven't been properly socialized as puppies.[3]

People can get "the big head" too. Maybe you know someone like that. What started off as self-confidence quickly turned into arrogance.

Maybe they even started trying to boss you around. You probably didn't like that much.

The Bible warns us to be careful about thinking we're something when we're not. It's not that we aren't important to God. We *all* are. But nobody wants to be around someone who is puffed up with pride and full of themselves. More important, we want to represent Christians in a way that brings glory to God.

Unleash the Truth: "Do not think of yourself more highly than you ought, but rather think of yourself with sober judgment." (Romans 12:3)

Digging Deeper: Do you know someone who has "the big head"? How does this person make you feel?

Fido 411: The Westie's cheerful personality and good looks have made it popular in advertising. Several large companies use Westies to represent their products. For example, a Westie is the mascot of the Cesar brand of dog food.

Weekly Tail-Waggers: Take time this week to do an attitude check—on yourself. Never mind anybody else, because the only person you can change is *you*. But take some time to honestly consider whether you might be thinking more of yourself than you should. Thank God for the gifts and abilities He's given you and ask Him to show you how you can use them to bring glory to Him.

Wendy

Whippet

Group Hound

Size 18 to 22 inches; 25 to 40 pounds

Origin The Whippet comes from England. In the 1800s, coal miners living in northern England loved to race dogs and hunt rabbits when they weren't working, but keeping large greyhounds proved expensive. Their solution was to breed a smaller version: the Whippet. The fast little dogs made their way to America in the early 1900s by way of textile workers who brought them across the ocean to Massachusetts.

A Whippet won Best in Show at Westminster in 1964.

AKC 1888

Do You Have Stereoscopic Vision?

According to some sources, the Whippet got its name from an old English expression, "whip it," which means "to go swiftly." Whether or not that's true is debatable, but one thing is for sure, this breed is one of the fastest in the world! Whippets can run up to 35 miles per hour![1]

Built for sprinting, Whippets aren't much for long-distance running. And, if you take them on a short walk in the winter, make sure you put a sweater on them. (They don't have much body fat so they get cold very easily.)

Here's something really unique about these quick canines: they are part of the sighthounds group, which means they hunt mainly by sight, not scent. They've been called "canine Ferraris" because of their incredible speed, but it's their ability to see clearly at any speed that makes this breed stand out. If a Whippet is chasing a rabbit, it can catch that rabbit with no problem because of the Whippet's stereoscopic vision, giving it a full range of sight and depth perception so it can see even the smallest movement. Its ability to see clearly in panoramic fashion—even at 35 mph—is astounding!

Wouldn't it be great if we had that same ability to see the big picture, no matter how fast we were plowing through life? Wouldn't it be awesome if we could see everything clearly in every situation? Well, we can't but here's some good news—God can! God sees our beginning and our ending all at once. The Bible says that He orders our steps so He knows exactly where we need to go and when we need to be there so that we don't miss any divine appointments or blessings. Though our vision might be limited, with God's guidance, we can stay on the right course and make the best decisions based on what He sees and His leading.

Unleash the Truth: "The Lord is watching everywhere, keeping his eye on both the evil and the good." (Proverbs 15:3 NLT)

Digging Deeper: Do you need to wear glasses? Does the world look differently when you don't wear them? It might be a little blurry or completely out of focus, right? Well, did you know you can become spiritually blind? It's true. If we don't trust God and stay close to Him and His guidance, we will not see things clearly and we will not make the best decisions.

Fido 411: Did you know that Whippets are one of the quietest breeds? They rarely bark.

Weekly Tail-Waggers: Ask God to help you see the big picture and not be distracted by things that aren't important. Pray:

Father God, help me to see things clearly through Your eyes. Help me to trust You more and keep my focus on You so that I can see the big picture of my life. In Jesus' mighty name. Amen.

Michelle

Wire Fox Terrier

Group: Terrier

Size: Up to 15.5 inches; 16 to 18 pounds

Origin: The Wire Fox Terrier is thought to be descended from the old Rough-coated Black and Tan Terrier of Wales and Northern England, crossed with a Smooth Fox Terrier. The Smooth Fox Terrier and the Wire Fox Terrier were considered two varieties of the same breed until 1984 when the AKC approved separate standards for each.[1]

The Wire Fox Terrier has taken Westminster's Best in Show title fifteen times and has earned the top spot in the terrier group twenty-four times. Wires are also fierce competitors in earthdog trials, agility, and obedience.[2]

AKC: 1885

Putting the Past Behind Us

The Wire Fox Terrier may be little and cute, but under all that cuteness beats the heart of a hunter. Originally carried in a pouch by mounted hunters, Wires were turned loose to flush out prey from underground. They chased foxes from their dens and made short work of groundhogs, rats, and other furry pests.[3]

These days Wires are better known as bosses in the show ring, but that doesn't mean they've lost their hunting instincts. Many Wires are active in earthdog trials, agility competitions, and hunting. These activities come with a risk of injury and sometimes result in battle scars. The AKC has special rules for Wires and other working dogs. Scars are not allowed to hurt their chances in the show ring. Scars are proof that Wires are working dogs and are not considered defects.[4]

Sometimes Christians have scars too. Maybe the scars are from past choices or from situations beyond our control like abuse or a dysfunctional family. But when we commit our lives to Jesus, things change. The Bible says we are made new. Yes, there may be some scars from the past, but God doesn't hold those against us. God accepts us just as we are. He heals our past hurts, and He can use our scars to help someone else who may be going through something similar. Because of what Jesus did on the cross, we are accepted and forgiven. Forget the past! God wants to do something new in you!

Unleash the Truth: "I focus on this one thing: Forgetting the past and looking forward to what lies ahead, I press on to reach the end of the race and receive the heavenly prize for which God, through Christ Jesus, is calling us." (Philippians 3:13b–14 NLT)

Digging Deeper: Consider this. Are you letting your past hold you back from the future God wants you to have? Are you letting guilt or past hurts keep you from experiencing God's total love and forgiveness? Can you identify what it is about the past that is bothering you?

Fido 411: A popular European comic book series of the 1900s, The Adventures of Tintin, included a white Wire named Snowy as the loyal sidekick to comic hero Tintin. Brave and fearless, Snowy frequently rescued Tintin from dangerous situations. The Adventures of Tintin was the inspiration for a 2011 Stephen Spielberg movie by the same name.[5]

Weekly Tail-Waggers: Once you've identified the things from your past that are troubling you, write them down. Put the list in an empty gift box. Then pray this prayer: "Father, I am Your child. I'm struggling with these things in my past. But now I'm giving them back to You. You can use them as You see fit. You can help me forget them. Or you can use them to help someone else. Let Your will be done in me. In Jesus' name. Amen." Put the box in your closet or under your bed. Leave it there. Then watch what God will do because you are letting go of your past and pressing on to finish your race!

Wendy

Yorkshire Terrier

Group Toy

Size 7 to 8 inches; 7 pounds

Origin The Yorkshire Terrier gets its name from Lancashire and Yorkshire counties in England where the breed began. It came from terrier mix breeds by way of Scotland migrants. This breed was first a working-class dog. It was bigger in size and was used to take care of rat problems in the coal mines and mills. In 1886 the Kennel Club of England recognized the breed, and it then became a lap dog. Yorkies came to America in the 1870s.

The Yorkie won Best in Show at Westminster in 1978.

AKC 1885

Barks of Bravery

The Yorkshire Terrier is almost always in the top ten of America's most popular breeds. Yorkies are adorable and full of personality! Because of their tiny bodies and long, silky hair, they've become known as little glamour girls, but that's not all they are! Yorkies were originally bred to chase after rats and other vermin in underground tunnels. (Yuck!) Yep, this little dog is a lot more than meets the eye! As it turns out, they're total tomboys!

Yorkies are also thought to be the first therapy dogs, visiting wounded soldiers in hospitals. A Yorkie named Smoky is even credited with saving the lives of many soldiers by dragging a communications cable through an eight-inch wide, sixty-foot long drainage culvert in World War II. There are six US-based memorials honoring Smoky, plus a book about her called *Yorkie*

Doodle Dandy written by Corporal William Wynne. These little dogs may look unassuming, but people turn to them to do brave and heroic acts.

Sometimes God will call upon you to do brave things too. Even if you feel like you're just the "glamour girl" or the "rat chaser," God has created you to be capable of so much more. When scary times come and you're called upon to be brave, remember that God is always with you. You don't have to be afraid because He will protect you. When you trust God and face your fears head-on, you can do some amazing things!

Unleash the Truth: "Be strong and courageous. Do not be afraid or terrified because of them, for the Lord your God goes with you; he will never leave you nor forsake you." (Deuteronomy 31:6)

Digging Deeper: Have you ever had to be brave? Do you feel confident today to tackle whatever God asks you to do?

Fido 411: The original drawings in the first edition of L. Frank Baum's book *The Wonderful Wizard of Oz* shows Toto as what most believe to be a Yorkie, which makes sense because the illustrator of the book (W. W. Denslow) owned a Yorkie. But, in the movie, Toto is played by a Cairn Terrier.[1]

Weekly Tail-Waggers: Create a list of people you think are brave. How have they shown bravery? What can you learn from these brave folks?

Michelle

Conclusion

I'm an only child. When I was a kid, people would always ask me, "Don't you want a little brother or little sister?"

My answer was always the same. "No, but I want a puppy."

I'm a firm believer that dogs are special animals. I really do believe that God uses all creation to point us toward Him. But dogs are especially good at it. In them we see so many things that speak to us of God's love and sometimes our own shortcomings. In many ways, our relationships with our dogs is much like our relationship with God. He's our Savior. We're theirs. He loves us. We love them. And so on.

The dogs in my life have taught me spiritual lessons on many occasions. They didn't know they were doing that. Or maybe they did. But I'm grateful to each one for showing me spiritual truths in ways that really spoke to me. And I hope I never forget the lessons. I pray I will always be the person my dogs seem to think I am.

And just so you know: Michelle and I wanted to write this book for two reasons. First, we love God, and we want kids to know and love Him, too. Second, we love dogs. We're both a bit crazy about them. And in the pages of this book, we've combined two of the things we love the most (except for our families, of course). Our prayer is that anyone, regardless of age, will find spiritual parallels and words of wisdom here that will deepen your walk with the Lord. We pray blessings upon you and that you may know and be known by the creator of all things—our heavenly Father.

Wendy

Dog Groups as Recognized by the American Kennel Club

Dog breeds are classified into groups by the Kennel Club, FCI (also known as the World Canine Organization), and the American Kennel Club. Dogs are assigned to a group based on their abilities and function.[1]

Herding Group: Dogs that excel at herding or guiding livestock such as sheep, cattle, goats, or ducks under the direction of a handler.

Hound Group: Dogs that are bred to pursue all kinds of warm-blooded quarry from rabbits to humans.

Non-Sporting Group: Dogs that do not fit into any other group are classified as non-sporting. Most are sought after as companion dogs.

Sporting Group: Dogs that are bred to assist hunters in capturing and retrieving feathered game.

Terrier Group: Dogs bred to go underground after rodents and other vermin or to locate and dig them out.

Toy Group: Dogs that are bred to serve as companions and lap dogs to humans.

Working Group: Dogs in this group include some of the oldest known breeds. They are bred to assist humans in some way including pulling carts and loads, guarding flocks and homes, and protecting families and individuals.

Glossary of Competition Terms

agility: A test of a dog's skill at negotiating a complex obstacle course composed of jumps, tunnels, seesaws, and bridges.

carting: An activity or contest in which a dog pulls a cart full of supplies and sometimes people.

companion events: Demonstrate how well a handler and dog work together.

conformation: An event in dog shows to determine the best specimens of the various AKC-recognized breeds.

drafting: This contest is similar to carting except the dog is harnessed to the cart between two shafts and cannot step from side to side.

earthdog: A test of a dog's ability to seek and locate prey underground; open only to small terriers and Dachshunds.

flyball: This sport matches two teams of four dogs each, racing side by side over a fifty-one-foot course. The dogs race relay style through a series of jumps, trigger a flyball box to release a ball, retrieve the ball, and return over the jumps.

freestyle: Also known as doggie dancing, this competition is a mixture of obedience training, tricks, and dance.

herding: A contest in which a dog uses its own abilities to move sheep (or other animals) around a field, fences, gates, or enclosures while taking directions from its handler.

lure coursing: A timed event in which a dog chases a mechanized lure as if it were chasing something in the wild.

nose work: Also called scent work, this is a contest in which a dog must locate a scent and communicate the find to the handler.

obedience: This event tests how well a dog and its handler work together by performing a series of obedience exercises including basics like *sit*, *down*, *heel*, and *stay*.

packing: An event that tests a dog's ability to carry a load over long distances.

pointing: For this event, a dog must locate game, point, and stand still for the gunshot once the game is flushed.

rally: Dog and handler teams negotiate a course of exercises following sequentially numbered signs called stations. The instructions for the exercises are written on signs at each station.

service dog: Dogs are trained to perform certain services for their owner and remain with them at all times. They serve as visual guide, hearing, diabetes alert, seizure response, mobility assistance, and allergy alert dogs, among many other specialties.

sledding: Teams of dogs race on marked courses including sprints and long-distance races.

therapy dogs: Dogs that work with their owners to provide emotional support in schools, hospitals, and nursing homes.

tracking: A test of a dog's ability to follow a scent while on a leash.

weight pulling: A contest in which a dog pulls a cart or sled loaded with weight across a short distance.

Note: Some breeds have their own competitions. Basset Hounds, Beagles, Coonhounds, and Dachshunds are all examples of breeds that have their own specific competitions. Other competitions such as field trials and scent hound field trials are open to select breeds.

Notes

Afghan Hound

[1] Unless a note says differently, all of the statistics for each breed have been verified at the website for the American Kennel Club, https://www.akc.org. The information about a breed's wins at Westminster is taken from the website for the Westminster Kennel Club Dog Show, https://www.westminsterkennelclub.org/.

[2] Rebecca O'Connell, "10 Elegant Facts About the Afghan Hound," Mental Floss, March 14, 2016, https://www.mentalfloss.com/article/76999/10-elegant-facts-about-afghan-hound.

Airedale Terrier

[1] T. J. Resler and Gary Weitzman, *Dog Breed Guide: A Complete Reference to Your Best Friend Fur-Ever* (Washington: National Geographic Children's Books, 2019), 224–25.

[2] Resler and Weitzman, *Dog Breed Guide*, 224.

Akita

[1] Kathryn Hennessy, ed., *The Dog Encyclopedia: The Definitive Visual Guide* (New York: DK, 2013), 111.

[2] Christopher Reggio, ed., *The New Complete Dog Book: Official Breed Standards and Profiles for Over 200 Breeds* (Mount Joy, PA: Fox Chapel, 2017), 302.

[3] "Group Records: Working," Westminster Kennel Club, accessed April 2, 2024, https://www.westminsterkennelclub.org/conformation-records/group-records/working/.

[4] Hennessy, *Dog Encyclopedia*, 111.

[5] Reggio, *New Complete Dog Book*, 302.

Alaskan Malamute

[1] Christopher Reggio, ed., *The New Complete Dog Book: Official Breed Standards and Profiles for Over 200 Breeds* (Mount Joy, PA: Fox Chapel, 2017), 306.

[2] "Group Records: Working," Westminster Kennel Club, accessed April 2, 2024, https://www.westminsterkennelclub.org/conformation-records/group-records/working/.

[3] Reggio, *New Complete Dog Book*, 307.

[4] Reggio, *New Complete Dog Book*, 307.

[5] "Alaskan Malamute," State Symbols USA, accessed May 7, 2020, https://statesymbolsusa.org/symbol/alaska/state-dog-or-cat-state-mammal/alaskan-malamute.

Notes

American English Coonhound
[1] Kathryn Hennessy, ed., *The Dog Encyclopedia: The Definitive Visual Guide* (New York: DK, 2013), 159.
[2] Christopher Reggio, ed., *The New Complete Dog Book: Official Breed Standards and Profiles for Over 200 Breeds* (Mount Joy, PA: Fox Chapel, 2017), 183.
[3] Hennessy, *Dog Encyclopedia*, 159.

American Eskimo Dog
[1] "American Eskimo Dog," American Kennel Club, https://www.akc.org/dog-breeds/american-eskimo-dog/#timeline.
[2] Kayla Fratt, "American Eskimo (Eskie): Dog Breed Profile," The Spruce Pets, October 2, 2019, https://www.thesprucepets.com/american-eskimo-dog-4584347.

American Foxhound
[1] Kathryn Hennessy, ed., *The Dog Encyclopedia: The Definitive Visual Guide* (New York: DK, 2013), 157.
[2] Christopher Reggio, ed., *The New Complete Dog Book: Official Breed Standards and Profiles for Over 200 Breeds* (Mount Joy, PA: Fox Chapel, 2017), 186.
[3] "Group Records: Hound," Westminster Kennel Club, accessed April 2, 2024, https://www.westminsterkennelclub.org/conformation-records/group-records/hound/.
[4] "American Foxhound Dog Breed Information," American Kennel Club, accessed May 12, 2021, https://www.akc.org/dog-breeds/american-foxhound/.
[5] "American Foxhound Dog Breed Information."

American Pit Bull Terrier
[1] "American Staffordshire Terrier," American Kennel Club, May 20, 2020, https://www.akc.org/dog-breeds/american-staffordshire-terrier/.

Australian Cattle Dog
[1] Christopher Reggio, ed., *The New Complete Dog Book: Official Breed Standards and Profiles for Over 200 Breeds* (Mount Joy, PA: Fox Chapel, 2017), 728.
[2] Kathryn Hennessy, ed., *The Dog Encyclopedia: The Definitive Visual Guide* (New York: DK, 2013), 62.
[3] Hennessy, *Dog Encyclopedia*, 63.
[4] Sanj Atwal, "World's Oldest Dog Ever, Bobi, Dies Aged 31," Guinness World Records, October 23, 2023, https://www.guinnessworldrecords.com/news/2023/10/worlds-oldest-dog-ever-bobi-dies-aged-31-760019.
[5] "Australian Cattle Dog," *Encyclopedia Britannica*, accessed February 23, 2020. https://www.britannica.com/animal/Australian-cattle-dog.

Notes

Australian Stumpy Tail Cattle Dog

[1] "The Purebred Australian Stumpy Tail Cattle Dog," Dog Breed Info, https://www.dogbreedinfo.com/stumpytailcattledog.htm.

[2] "Rutland Deceased K-9 Officer Recognized," WNTK Breaking News, https://wntk.wordpress.com/2016/05/24/rutland-deceased-k-9-officer-recognized/.

Basenji

[1] Aastha, "37 Interesting Facts About Basenjis," DogCrunch, last modified March 16, 2020, https://dogcrunch.com/interesting-facts-about-basenjis/.

[2] "Group Records: Hound," Westminster Kennel Club, accessed April 2, 2024, https://www.westminsterkennelclub.org/conformation-records/group-records/hound/.

[3] Christopher Reggio, ed., *The New Complete Dog Book: Official Breed Standards and Profiles for Over 200 Breeds* (Mount Joy, PA: Fox Chapel, 2017), 191.

[4] Kathryn Hennessy, ed., *The Dog Encyclopedia: The Definitive Visual Guide* (New York: DK, 2013), 31.

[5] Aastha, "37 Interesting Facts About Basenjis."

Beagle

[1] Christopher Reggio, ed., *The New Complete Dog Book: Official Breed Standards and Profiles for Over 200 Breeds* (Mount Joy, PA: Fox Chapel, 2017), 198.

[2] "Group Records: Hound," Westminster Kennel Club, accessed April 2, 2024, https://www.westminsterkennelclub.org/conformation-records/group-records/hound/.

[3] Rebecca O'Connell, "10 Howling Good Facts About Beagles," Mental Floss, last modified June 16, 2015, https://www.mentalfloss.com/article/65033/10-howling-good-facts-about-beagles.

[4] Reggio, *New Complete Dog Book*, 199.

[5] O'Connell, "10 Howling Good Facts About Beagles."

Bearded Collie

[1] Nancy Hajeski, *Every Dog: A Book of Over 450 Dog Breeds* (Ontario: Firefly, 2016).

[2] "Group Records: Herding," Westminster Kennel Club, accessed April 2, 2024, https://www.westminsterkennelclub.org/conformation-records/group-records/herding/.

Belgian Malinois

[1] "Five Heroic Dogs Honored with AKC Humane Fund Awards for Canine Excellence (ACE)," American Kennel Club, October 7, 2015, https://www.akc.org/press-releases/five-heroic-dogs-honored-with-akc-humane-fund-awards-for-canine-excellence-ace/.

Bernese Mountain Dog

[1] Kathryn Hennessy, ed., *The Dog Encyclopedia: The Definitive Visual Guide* (New York: DK, 2013), 73.

Notes

[2] "Group Records: Working," Westminster Kennel Club, accessed April 2, 2024, https://www.westminsterkennelclub.org/conformation-records/group-records/working/.

[3] Christopher Reggio, ed., *The New Complete Dog Book: Official Breed Standards and Profiles for Over 200 Breeds* (Mount Joy, PA: Fox Chapel, 2017), 315.

[4] "Gallery of Grand Master Draft Dogs," Bernese Mountain Dog Club of America, last modified August 24, 2014, https://www.bmdca.org/Draft/cs_gallery.php.

[5] Hennessy, *Dog Encyclopedia*, 73.

[6] Hennessy, *Dog Encyclopedia*. 73.

Bichon Frise

[1] Christopher Reggio, ed., *The New Complete Dog Book: Official Breed Standards and Profiles for Over 200 Breeds* (Mount Joy, PA: Fox Chapel, 2017), 642.

[2] "Group Records: Non-Sporting," Westminster Kennel Club, accessed April 2, 2024, https://www.westminsterkennelclub.org/conformation-records/group-records/non-sporting/.

[3] Reggio, *New Complete Dog Book*, 642–43.

[4] Reggio, *New Complete Dog Book*, 642.

[5] Reggio, *New Complete Dog Book*, 642–43.

[6] Reggio, *New Complete Dog Book*, 643.

Bloodhound

[1] "2018 ACE Award Winners: Meet the 5 Heroic Dogs Being Honored This Year," American Kennel Club, August 23, 2018, https://www.akc.org/expert-advice/news/ace-award-winners-2018/.

Border Collie

[1] Christopher Reggio, ed., *The New Complete Dog Book: Official Breed Standards and Profiles for Over 200 Breeds* (Mount Joy, PA: Fox Chapel, 2017), 764.

[2] Jennifer Peltz, "In the Pink: Border Collie Wins Westminster Agility Contest," *Washington Post*, last modified February 8, 2020, https://www.washingtonpost.com/sports/in-the-pink-border-collie-wins-westminster-agility-contest/2020/02/08/283a2afe-4ae3-11ea-8a1f-de1597be6cbc_story.html.

[3] Reggio, *New Complete Dog Book*, 764.

[4] Kathryn Hennessy, ed., *The Dog Encyclopedia: The Definitive Visual Guide* (New York: DK, 2013), 51.

[5] Hennessy, *Dog Encyclopedia*, 51.

Notes

Boston Terrier

[1] "All About Stubby," Sergeant Stubby Salutes, last modified August 9, 2018, https://sergeantstubbysalutes.org/?page_id=2417.

[2] Rebecca O'Connell, "9 Fun Facts About Boston Terriers," Mental Floss, October 28, 2018, https://www.mentalfloss.com/article/65827/9-frisky-facts-about-boston-terriers.

[3] "Boston Terrier," American Kennel Club, https://www.akc.org/dog-breeds/boston-terrier/.

Boxer

[1] Christopher Reggio, ed., *The New Complete Dog Book: Official Breed Standards and Profiles for Over 200 Breeds* (Mount Joy, PA: Fox Chapel, 2017), 326.

[2] "Group Records: Working," Westminster Kennel Club, accessed April 2, 2024, https://www.westminsterkennelclub.org/conformation-records/group-records/working/.

[3] Reggio, *New Complete Dog Book*, 326–27.

[4] Lawrence Robinson, Melinda Smith, and Jeanne Segal, "Laughter Is the Best Medicine," HelpGuide.org, last modified February 16, 2020, https://www.helpguide.org/articles/mental-health/laughter-is-the-best-medicine.htm.

[5] Robinson, Smith, and Segal, "Laughter Is the Best Medicine," 327.

Bull Terrier

[1] Kathryn Hennessy, ed., *The Dog Encyclopedia: The Definitive Visual Guide* (New York: DK, 2013), 197.

[2] "Group Records: Terrier," Westminster Kennel Club, accessed April 2, 2024, https://www.westminsterkennelclub.org/conformation-records/group-records/terrier/.

[3] Rebecca O'Connell, "9 Solid Facts About Bull Terriers," Mental Floss, last modified August 31, 2015, https://www.mentalfloss.com/article/67941/9-solid-facts-about-bull-terriers.

[4] O'Connell, "9 Solid Facts About Bull Terriers."

Bulldog

[1] Christopher Reggio, ed., *The New Complete Dog Book: Official Breed Standards and Profiles for Over 200 Breeds* (Mount Joy, PA: Fox Chapel, 2017), 650.

[2] "Group Records: Non-Sporting," Westminster Kennel Club, accessed April 2, 2024, https://www.westminsterkennelclub.org/conformation-records/group-records/non-sporting/.

[3] Danielle Garrand, "'Thor' the Bulldog Wins Best in Show at 2019 National Dog Show," CBS News, last modified November 28, 2019, https://www.cbsnews.com/news/national-dog-show-2019-thor-bulldog-wins-best-in-show-2019-national-dog-show/.

Notes

[4] Winston Churchill, speech to Harrow School, October 29, 1941, https://www.nationalchurchillmuseum.org/never-give-in-never-never-never.html.

[5] "Otto the Skateboarding Bulldog," *Guinness World Records*, accessed February 27, 2020, https://guinnessworldrecords.com/records/hall-of-fame/otto-the-skateboarding-bulldog/.

Bullmastiff

[1] Christopher Reggio, ed., *The New Complete Dog Book: Official Breed Standards and Profiles for Over 200 Breeds* (Mount Joy, PA: Fox Chapel, 2017), 332.

[2] "Group Records: Working," Westminster Kennel Club, accessed April 2, 2024, https://www.westminsterkennelclub.org/conformation-records/group-records/working/.

[3] Reggio, *New Complete Dog Book*, 333.

[4] Reggio, *New Complete Dog Book*, 332.

[5] Reggio, *New Complete Dog Book*, 332.

Cairn Terrier

[1] Christopher Reggio, ed., *The New Complete Dog Book: Official Breed Standards and Profiles for Over 200 Breeds* (Mount Joy, PA: Fox Chapel, 2017), 454.

[2] "Group Records: Terrier," Westminster Kennel Club, accessed April 2, 2024, https://www.westminsterkennelclub.org/conformation-records/group-records/terrier/.

[3] Reggio, *New Complete Dog Book*, 454.

Cane Corso

[1] "Cane Corso," American Kennel Club, accessed February 11, 2024, https://www.akc.org/dog-breeds/cane-corso/.

[2] "Corsos for Heroes Non-Profit Provides Veterans, First Responders Comfort with Service Dogs," FOX 13 Tampa Bay, May 5, 2023, https://www.fox13news.com/news/corsos-for-heroes-non-profit-provides-dogs-for-veterans.

[3] Jamie L. LaReau, "Michigan Teen and Her Cane Corso Dog Win a Title at Westminster Dog Show," *Detroit Free Press*, May 10, 2023, https://www.freep.com/story/news/local/michigan/2023/05/10/michigan-teen-and-her-dog-win-a-title-at-westminster-dog-show/70201490007/.

Catahoula Leopard Dog

[1] "Catahoula Leopard Dog," Daily Paws, last modified August 24, 2020, https://www.dailypaws.com/dogs-puppies/dog-breeds/catahoula-leopard-dog.

Chesapeake Bay Retriever

[1] Christopher Reggio, ed., *The New Complete Dog Book: Official Breed Standards and Profiles for Over 200 Breeds* (Mount Joy, PA: Fox Chapel, 2017), 62–63.

[2] "Group Records: Sporting," Westminster Kennel Club, accessed April 2, 2024, https://www.westminsterkennelclub.org/conformation-records/group-records/sporting/.

[3] Reggio, *New Complete Dog Book*, 63.

[4] Reggio, *New Complete Dog Book*, 63.

[5] Denise Flaim, "Chesapeake Bay Retriever History: America's Water Dog," American Kennel Club, last modified April 6, 2021, https://www.akc.org/expert-advice/dog-breeds/chesapeake-bay-retriever-history-americas-water-dog/.

Chihuahua

[1] Heather M., "Facts About Chihuahuas," ASPCA Pet Health Insurance, https://www.aspcapetinsurance.com/blog/2016/may/30/facts-about-chihuahuas/.

Chinese Crested

[1] Nancy Hajeski, *Every Dog: A Book of 500 Breeds* (Richmond Hill, Ontario: Firefly, 2016), 474. Also see per the chinesecrestedclubinfo.com/club-history.

[2] "Chinese Crested," Dogtime, https://dogtime.com/dog-breeds/chinese-crested#/slide/.

Chinese Shar-Pei

[1] Christopher Reggio, ed., *The New Complete Dog Book: Official Breed Standards and Profiles for Over 200 Breeds* (Mount Joy, PA: Fox Chapel, 2017), 656.

[2] "Group Records: Non-Sporting," Westminster Kennel Club, accessed April 2, 2024, https://www.westminsterkennelclub.org/conformation-records/group-records/nonsporting/.

[3] Reggio, *New Complete Dog Book*, 657.

[4] Reggio, *New Complete Dog Book*, 656–57.

[5] Katherine Ripley, "7 Things You Didn't Know About the Chinese Shar-Pei," American Kennel Club, last modified September 1, 2016, https://www.akc.org/expert-advice/lifestyle/7-things-you-didnt-know-about-the-chinese-shar-pei/.

Chow Chow

[1] Celebrities Category, chowtales.com/category/celebrity-chows/.

[2] Rebecca O'Connell, "11 Fluffy Facts About Chow Chows," Mental Floss, February 1, 2016, https://www.mentalfloss.com/article/74605/11-fluffy-facts-about-chow-chows.

Cocker Spaniel

[1] "What Breed of Dog Is Lady from 'Lady and the Tramp'?," Reference, April 1, 2020, https://www.reference.com/pets-animals/breed-dog-lady-lady-tramp-c8fad0f46937f531.

Collie

[1] Christopher Reggio, ed., *The New Complete Dog Book: Official Breed Standards and Profiles for Over 200 Breeds* (Mount Joy, PA: Fox Chapel, 2017), 784–85.

[2] "Group Records: Herding," Westminster Kennel Club, accessed April 2, 2024, https://www.westminsterkennelclub.org/conformation-records/group-records/herding/.

[3] Reggio, *New Complete Dog Book*, 784.

Czechoslovakian Vlcak

[1] "Czechoslovakian Vlcak Dog Breed Information," American Kennel Club, accessed March 8, 2021, https://www.akc.org/dog-breeds/czechoslovakian-vlcak.

[2] "Czechoslovakian Vlcak Dog Breed Information."

Dachshund

[1] Barri Segal, "You'll Never Guess Which Popular Dog Breeds Have Never Won Best in Show," Showbiz Cheat Sheet, May 22, 2018, https://www.cheatsheet.com/culture/youll-never-guess-which-popular-dog-breeds-have-never-won-best-in-show.html/.

[2] Ava Jaine, "Origin of the Dachshund," Dachshund Station, January 15, 2021, https://www.dachshundstation.com/origin/.

[3] Nancy Hajeski, *Every Dog: A Book of 500 Breeds* (Richmond Hill, Ontario: Firefly, 2016), 82.

Dalmatian

[1] Christopher Reggio, ed., *The New Complete Dog Book: Official Breed Standards and Profiles for Over 200 Breeds* (Mount Joy, PA: Fox Chapel, 2017), 672.

[2] Reggio, *New Complete Dog Book*, 673.

[3] Kathryn Hennessy, ed., *The Dog Encyclopedia: The Definitive Visual Guide* (New York: DK, 2013), 286.

[4] Rebecca O'Connell, "11 Spotted Facts About Dalmatians," Mental Floss, last modified March 29, 2016, https://www.mentalfloss.com/article/66339/11-spotted-facts-about-dalmatians.

Doberman Pinscher

[1] Carlotta Cooper, "Doberman Pinscher," Pawster, https://pawster.com/doberman-pinscher/.

French Bulldog

[1] Christopher Reggio, ed., *The New Complete Dog Book: Official Breed Standards and Profiles for Over 200 Breeds* (Mount Joy, PA: Fox Chapel, 2017), 680.

[2] Reggio, *New Complete Dog Book*, 681.

Notes

[3] Kathryn Hennessy, ed., *The Dog Encyclopedia: The Definitive Visual Guide* (New York: DK, 2013), 267.

[4] Rebecca O'Connell, "11 Facts About French Bulldogs," Mental Floss, last modified November 18, 2018, https://www.mentalfloss.com/article/63568/11-charming-facts-about-french-bulldogs.

German Shepherd

[1] T. J. Resler, and Gary Weitzman, *Dog Breed Guide: A Complete Reference to Your Best Friend Furr-Ever* (Washington, DC: National Geographic Children's Books, 2019), 176.

[2] "Q: How Many Times Has a German Shepherd Won Best in Show at the Westminster Kennel Club Dog Show?," Good News for Pets, February 15, 2017, https://goodnewsforpets.com/german-shepherd-best-show-westminster-kennel-club-dog-show/.

[3] Rebecca O'Connell, "10 Noble Facts About German Shepherds," Mental Floss, June 1, 2015, https://www.mentalfloss.com/article/64533/10-noble-facts-about-german-shepherds.

[4] Merriam-Webster Learner's Dictionary, s.v. "loyal," https://www.learnersdictionary.com/definition/Loyal.

German Shorthaired Pointer

[1] "German Shorthaired Pointer—Did You Know?," American Kennel Club, https://www.akc.org/dog-breeds/german-shorthaired-pointer/.

Golden Retriever

[1] Christopher Reggio, ed., *The New Complete Dog Book: Official Breed Standards and Profiles for Over 200 Breeds* (Mount Joy, PA: Fox Chapel, 2017), 108.

[2] Nicole L. Pesce, "'The Golden Retriever Was Robbed!' Many Dog Lovers Disappointed That a Poodle Won Westminster—Again," MarketWatch, last modified February 13, 2020, https://www.marketwatch.com/story/the-golden-retriever-was-robbed-many-dog-lovers-disappointed-that-a-poodle-won-westminster-again-2020-02-12.

[3] Kathryn Hennessy, ed., *The Dog Encyclopedia: The Definitive Visual Guide* (New York: DK, 2013), 259.

[4] Hennessy, *Dog Encyclopedia*, 259.

[5] Alex Lasker, "Golden Retriever Breaks World Record for Most Tennis Balls Held in Mouth at Once," AOL.com, last modified February 13, 2020, https://www.aol.com/article/lifestyle/2020/02/13/golden-retriever-breaks-world-record-for-most-tennis-balls-held-in-mouth-at-once/23925623/.

Goldendoodle

[1] "Goldendoodle," Dog Time, https://dogtime.com/dog-breeds/goldendoodle#/slide/1.

[2] Kathryn Hennessy, ed., *The Dog Encyclopedia: The Definitive Visual Guide* (New York: DK, 2013), 294.

Notes

[3] Hennessy, *Dog Encyclopedia*, 294.

[4] Hennessy, *Dog Encyclopedia*, 294.

[5] Janet Tran, "8 Pawesome Goldendoodle Facts You Didn't Know," BarkForce, last modified April 8, 2020, https://barkforce.com/8-pawesome-goldendoodle-facts-didnt-know.

Great Dane

[1] Christopher Reggio, ed., *The New Complete Dog Book: Official Breed Standards and Profiles for Over 200 Breeds* (Mount Joy, PA: Fox Chapel, 2017), 360.

[2] "Group Records: Working," Westminster Kennel Club, accessed April 2, 2024, https://www.westminsterkennelclub.org/conformation-records/group-records/working/.

[3] Reggio, *New Complete Dog Book*, 361.

[4] "10 Things You Might Not Know About Great Danes," Rocky Mountain Great Dane Rescue, Inc., last modified December 22, 2014, https://rmgreatdane.org/10-things-might-not-know-great-danes/.

[5] Ellen Castelow, "Able Seaman Just Nuisance," Historic UK, last modified September 20, 2016, https://www.historic-uk.com/HistoryUK/HistoryofBritain/Able-Seaman-Just-Nuisance/.

Great Pyrenees

[1] "Great Pyrenees," DogTime, last modified January 22, 2024, https://dogtime.com/dog-breeds/great-pyrenees.

Greyhound

[1] Kelli Bender, "Gia the Greyhound Wins Best in Show at 15th Annual National Dog Show Presented by Purina," *People*, November 24, 2016, https://people.com/pets/gia-the-greyhound-wins-best-in-show-at-15th-annual-national-dog-show-presented-by-purina/.

Ibizan Hound

[1] Christopher Reggio, ed., *The New Complete Dog Book: Official Breed Standards and Profiles for Over 200 Breeds* (Mount Joy, PA: Fox Chapel, 2017), 240.

[2] "Group Records: Hound," Westminster Kennel Club, accessed April 2, 2024, https://www.westminsterkennelclub.org/conformation-records/group-records/hound/.

[3] Reggio, *New Complete Dog Book*, 241.

[4] Reggio, *New Complete Dog Book*, 241.

[5] Ranny Green, "A Dog of Many Talents: Meet a Grand Champion Ibizan Hound Who Is Also a Service Dog," American Kennel Club, last modified July 7, 2016, https://www.akc.org/expert-advice/news/grand-champion-ibizan-hound-also-service-dog/.

Notes

Irish Setter

[1] Michele Welton, "Irish Setters: What's Good About 'Em, What's Bad About 'Em," Your Purebred Puppy, https://www.yourpurebredpuppy.com/reviews/irishsetters.html.

Irish Wolfhound

[1] Christopher Reggio, ed., *The New Complete Dog Book: Official Breed Standards and Profiles for Over 200 Breeds* (Mount Joy, PA: Fox Chapel, 2017), 244.

[2] "Group Records: Hound," Westminster Kennel Club, accessed April 2, 2024, https://www.westminsterkennelclub.org/conformation-records/group-records/hound/.

[3] Katherine Ripley, "Irish Wolfhound Facts: 9 Things to Know About This Giant Dog Breed," American Kennel Club, last modified May 26, 2023, https://www.akc.org/expert-advice/lifestyle/didnt-know-about-irish-wolfhound/.

[4] Reggio, *New Complete Dog Book*, 244.

[5] Ripley, "Irish Wolfhound Facts."

Japanese Chin

[1] Christopher Reggio, ed., *The New Complete Dog Book: Official Breed Standards and Profiles for Over 200 Breeds* (Mount Joy, PA: Fox Chapel, 2017), 584–85.

[2] "Japanese Chin," Dogtime, https://dogtime.com/dog-breeds/japanese-chin#/slide/1.

Keeshond

[1] Christopher Reggio, ed., *The New Complete Dog Book: Official Breed Standards and Profiles for Over 200 Breeds* (Mount Joy, PA: Fox Chapel, 2017), 684.

[2] "Group Records: Non-sporting," Westminster Kennel Club, accessed April 2, 2024, https://www.westminsterkennelclub.org/conformation-records/group-records/non-sporting/.

[3] Reggio, *New Complete Dog Book*, 685.

[4] Reggio, *New Complete Dog Book*, 684.

[5] Mara Bovsun, "7 Reasons Why the Keeshond Totally Owns the Nickname the Smiling Dutchman—American Kennel Club," American Kennel Club, last modified December 3, 2015, https://www.akc.org/expert-advice/lifestyle/7-reasons-why-keeshond-owns-nickname/.

Komondor

[1] Christopher Reggio, ed., *The New Complete Dog Book: Official Breed Standards and Profiles for Over 200 Breeds* (Mount Joy, PA: Fox Chapel, 2017), 372–75.

[2] "Group Records: Working," Westminster Kennel Club, accessed April 2, 2024, https://www.westminsterkennelclub.org/conformation-records/group-records/working/.

Notes

[3] Kathryn Hennessy, ed., *The Dog Encyclopedia: The Definitive Visual Guide* (New York: DK, 2013), 66–67.

Labradoodle

[1] "Labradoodle," Dog Time, accessed February 15, 2024, https://dogtime.com/dog-breeds/labradoodle.

[2] Kathryn Hennessy, ed., *The Dog Encyclopedia: The Definitive Visual Guide* (New York: DK, 2013), 291.

[3] Heather Logue, "12 Facts Only Labradoodle People Understand," Rover.com, accessed January 20, 2024, https://www.rover.com/blog/labradoodle-facts/.

[4] Logue, "12 Facts Only Labradoodle People Understand."

[5] Bethany Bailey, phone interview with author, March 3, 2023.

[6] Hennessy, *Dog Encyclopedia*, 291.

Labrador Retriever

[1] Anneta Konstantinides, "16 Dog Breeds That Have Never Won the Westminster Dog Show," Insider, February 5, 2020, https://www.insider.com/dog-breeds-that-have-never-won-westminster-dog-show-2020-2.

[2] James Crabtree-Hannigan, "Who Won the Westminster Dog Show in 2020? Breed Results, Group Winners & Best in Show," Sporting News, February 14, 2020, https://www.sportingnews.com/us/other-sports/news/westminster-dog-show-2020-live-results-best-in-show/1vq0x97q38h0i1a4x7xdehm454.

[3] Rebecca O'Connell, "12 Friendly Facts About Labrador Retrievers," Mental Floss, May 11, 2015, https://www.mentalfloss.com/article/63891/12-friendly-facts-about-labrador-retrievers.

Maremma Sheepdog

[1] "Official American Standard for the Maremma Sheepdog," Maremma Sheepdog Club of America, http://www.maremmaclub.com/standard.html.

[2] "Maremma Sheepdog," Europetnet, accessed February 19, 2020, https://www.europetnet.com/pet-resources/dog-breeds/item/1720-maremma-sheepdog.html.

[3] Kathryn Hennessy, ed., *The Dog Encyclopedia: The Definitive Visual Guide* (New York: DK, 2013), 69.

[4] Emma Nobel, "Hero Penguin Protector Dog Retires After Almost a Decade of Service," ABC News, last modified October 17, 2019, https://www.abc.net.au/news/2019-10-17/middle-island-penguin-protector-oddball-maremma-retires/11607662.

Mixed Breed

[1] Kathryn Hennessy, ed., *The Dog Encyclopedia: The Definitive Visual Guide* (New York: DK, 2013), 298.

[2] Hennessy, *Dog Encyclopedia*, 298.

Newfoundland

[1] Kathryn Hennessy, ed., *The Dog Encyclopedia: The Definitive Visual Guide* (New York: DK, 2013), 79.

[2] "Group Records: Working," Westminster Kennel Club, accessed April 2, 2024, https://www.westminsterkennelclub.org/conformation-records/group-records/working/.

[3] Christopher Reggio, ed., *The New Complete Dog Book: Official Breed Standards and Profiles for Over 200 Breeds* (Mount Joy, PA: Fox Chapel, 2017), 392–93.

[4] Patti R. Eubank, *Seaman's Journal: On the Trail with Lewis and Clark* (Nashville: Ideals, 2002).

[5] Eubank, *Seaman's Journal*.

[6] Reggio, *New Complete Dog Book*, 393.

Old English Sheepdog

[1] Christopher Reggio, ed., *The New Complete Dog Book: Official Breed Standards and Profiles for Over 200 Breeds* (Mount Joy, PA: Fox Chapel, 2017), 816.

[2] "Group Records: Herding," Westminster Kennel Club, accessed April 2, 2024, https://www.westminsterkennelclub.org/conformation-records/group-records/herding/.

[3] Reggio, *New Complete Dog Book*, 817.

[4] Reggio, *New Complete Dog Book*, 817.

[5] Reggio, *New Complete Dog Book*, 816.

Papillon

[1] Christopher Reggio, ed., *The New Complete Dog Book: Official Breed Standards and Profiles for Over 200 Breeds* (Mount Joy, PA: Fox Chapel, 2017), 600.

[2] "Group Records: Toy," Westminster Kennel Club, accessed April 2, 2024, https://www.westminsterkennelclub.org/conformation-records/group-records/toy/.

[3] Reggio, *New Complete Dog Book*, 601.

[4] Rebecca O'Connell, "10 Fancy Facts About the Papillon," Mental Floss, last modified May 11, 2016, https://www.mentalfloss.com/article/79608/10-fancy-facts-about-papillon.

[5] O'Connell, "10 Fancy Facts About the Papillon."

Parson Russell Terrier

[1] Christopher Reggio, ed., *The New Complete Dog Book: Official Breed Standards and Profiles for Over 200 Breeds* (Mount Joy, PA: Fox Chapel, 2017), 502.

[2] Reggio, *New Complete Dog Book*, 502.

Pekingese

[3] Nancy Hajeski, *Every Dog: A Book of 450 Breeds* (Richmond Hill, Ontario: Firefly, 2016), 493.

[4] Hajeski, *Every Dog*, 493.

Notes

Pembroke Welsh Corgi

[1] Anneta Konstantinides, "16 Dog Breeds That Have Never Won the Westminster Dog Show," Insider, February 5, 2020, https://www.insider.com/dog-breeds-that-have-never-won-westminster-dog-show-2020-2.

Pomeranian

[1] "Pomeranian," under "History," Petfinder, https://www.petfinder.com/dog-breeds/pomeranian.

[2] "Pomeranian," Dogtime, https://dogtime.com/dog-breeds/pomeranian#/slide/1.

Poodle

[1] "Poodle (Standard)," American Kennel Club, https://www.akc.org/dog-breeds/poodle-standard/.

[2] Kelly Wilson, "Poodle Breed Information: Temperament, Health, and Sizes (Standard, Miniature, Toy)," Love Your Dog, October 22, 2020, https://www.loveyourdog.com/poodles/.

Pug

[1] Wendy H. Lanier, *Pugs* (Mankato, MN: Focus Readers, 2018), 9.

[2] "Group Records: Toy," Westminster Kennel Club, accessed April 2, 2024, https://www.westminsterkennelclub.org/conformation-records/group-records/toy/.

[3] American Kennel Club, *The New Complete Dog Book: Official Breed Standards and All-New Profiles for 200 Breeds*, 21st ed. (Irvine, CA: i-5 Press, 2015), 609.

[4] Kristy Beck, "The Importance of Cleaning Your Pug's Wrinkles," The Pug Diary, last modified March 20, 2018, https://www.thepugdiary.com/the-importance-of-cleaning-your-pugs-wrinkles/.

Puggle

[1] "Puggle," https://dogtime.com/dog-breeds/puggle#/slide/1.

[2] Kathryn Hennessy, ed., *The Dog Encyclopedia: The Definitive Visual Guide* (New York: DK, 2013), 297.

[3] Emily Green, "Everything You Need to Know About the Puggle," Doggie Designer, last modified February 19, 2020, https://doggiedesigner.com/puggle-complete-guide/.

[4] Bojana Radulovik, "15 Amazing Facts About Puggle," Barking Royalty, last modified July 11, 2019, https://barkingroyalty.com/puggle/.

Puli

[1] Becky Peterson and Paige Leskin, "The Adorable Dogs Owned by the Most Powerful Tech Executives, from Mark Zuckerberg to Elon Musk," Insider, https://www.businessinsider.com/tech-industry-titans-dogs-2017-6.

Notes

Rat Terrier
[1] Christopher Reggio, ed., *The New Complete Dog Book: Official Breed Standards and Profiles for Over 200 Breeds* (Mount Joy, PA: Fox Chapel, 2017), 506.

[2] "Group Records: Terrier," Westminster Kennel Club, accessed April 2, 2024, https://www.westminsterkennelclub.org/conformation-records/group-records/terrier/.

[3] Reggio, *New Complete Dog Book*, 507.

[4] Reggio, *New Complete Dog Book*, 508.

[5] Leah Bitsky, "Meet the Fearless Dogs Solving NYC's Rat Problem," *New York Post*, last modified March 23, 2017, https://nypost.com/2017/03/23/these-fearless-pups-thirst-for-rat-blood/.

Rottweiler
[1] "10 Fun Facts About Rottweilers," Rottweilers Online, https://www.rottweilersonline.com/general/10-fun-facts-about-rottweilers.

Russian Toy
[1] Kathryn Hennessy, ed., *The Dog Encyclopedia: The Definitive Visual Guide* (New York: DK, 2013), 275.

[2] Hennessy, *Dog Encyclopedia*, 275.

[3] Hennessy, *Dog Encyclopedia*, 275.

Saint Bernard
[1] Christopher Reggio, ed., *The New Complete Dog Book: Official Breed Standards and Profiles for Over 200 Breeds* (Mount Joy, PA: Fox Chapel, 2017), 404.

[2] "Group Records: Working," Westminster Kennel Club, accessed April 2, 2024, https://www.westminsterkennelclub.org/conformation-records/group-records/working/.

[3] Reggio, *New Complete Dog Book*, 404.

[4] "History of Saint Bernards," The Saint Bernard Club Inc., accessed May 1, 2020, https://www.stbernard.org.au/history-of-saint-bernards.html.

[5] Kathryn Hennessy, ed., *The Dog Encyclopedia: The Definitive Visual Guide* (New York: DK, 2013), 76.

Samoyed
[1] Christopher Reggio, ed., *The New Complete Dog Book: Official Breed Standards and Profiles for Over 200 Breeds* (Mount Joy, PA: Fox Chapel, 2017), 408.

[2] "Group Records: Working," Westminster Kennel Club, accessed April 2, 2024, https://www.westminsterkennelclub.org/conformation-records/group-records/working/.

[3] Reggio, *New Complete Dog Book*, 409.

Notes

[4] Kathryn Hennessy, ed., *The Dog Encyclopedia: The Definitive Visual Guide* (New York: DK, 2013), 106.

[5] Hennessy, *Dog Encyclopedia*, 106.

[6] Hennessy, *Dog Encyclopedia*, 106.

Schipperke

[1] Christopher Reggio, ed., *The New Complete Dog Book: Official Breed Standards and Profiles for Over 200 Breeds* (Mount Joy, PA: Fox Chapel, 2017), 706.

[2] "Group Records: Non-Sporting," Westminster Kennel Club, accessed April 2, 2024, https://www.westminsterkennelclub.org/conformation-records/group-records/non-sporting/.

[3] Reggio, *New Complete Dog Book*, 707.

[4] Reggio, *New Complete Dog Book*, 707.

[5] "Schipperke—Fun Facts and Crate Size," Pet Crates Direct, last modified June 23, 2019, https://www.petcratesdirect.com/blogs/news/schipperke-fun-facts-and-crate-size.

Scottish Deerhound

[1] T. J. Resler and Gary Weitzman, *Dog Breed Guide: A Complete Reference to Your Best Friend Fur-Ever* (Washington: National Geographic Children's Books, 2019), 122.

[2] "A Country Dog Charms the Big Show in the City," *New York Times*, February 16, 2011, https://www.nytimes.com/2011/02/16/sports/16best.html.

[3] Nancy J. Hajeski, *Every Dog: A Book of Over 450 Breeds* (Richmond Hill, Ontario: Firefly, 2016), 46.

Scottish Terrier

[1] "Scottish Terrier," Petfinder, accessed May 20, 2020, https://www.petfinder.com/dog-breeds/scottish-terrier/.

[2] "The Dog Breeds with the Most Wins at the Westminster Dog Show," *Reader's Digest*, January 28, 2020, https://www.rd.com/advice/pets/breeds-with-the-most-wins-at-the-westminster-dog-show/.

[3] "Scottish Terrier," American Kennel Club, https://www.akc.org/dog-breeds/scottish-terrier/.

[4] "Top Dogs at the White House," The White House Historical Association, https://www.whitehousehistory.org/white-house-pets/top-dogs-at-the-white-house.

Shetland Sheepdog (Shelties)

[1] Michele Welton, "Shetland Sheepdogs: What's Good About 'Em, What's Bad About 'Em," Your Purebred Puppy, https://www.yourpurebredpuppy.com/reviews/shelties.html.

Notes

Shih Tzu

[1] Molly, "Are Shih Tzu Better In Pairs?," Everything Shih Tzu, April 1, 2019, https://www.everythingshihtzu.com/are-shih-tzu-better-in-pairs.html.

Siberian Husky

[1] Christopher Reggio, ed., *The New Complete Dog Book: Official Breed Standards and Profiles for Over 200 Breeds* (Mount Joy, PA: Fox Chapel, 2017), 412.
[2] "Group Records: Working," Westminster Kennel Club, accessed April 2, 2024, https://www.westminsterkennelclub.org/conformation-records/group-records/working/.
[3] Reggio, *New Complete Dog Book*, 413
[4] Kathryn Hennessy, ed., *The Dog Encyclopedia: The Definitive Visual Guide* (New York: DK, 2013), 101.
[5] Hennessy, *Dog Encyclopedia*, 101.
[6] Hennessy, *Dog Encyclopedia*, 101.

Soft Coated Wheaten Terrier

[1] Jan Reisen, "6 Fun Facts About the Soft Coated Wheaten Terrier," American Kennel Club, last modified September 28, 2022, https://www.akc.org/expert-advice/lifestyle/soft-coated-wheaten-terrier-facts/.

Weimaraner

[1] Christopher Reggio, ed., *The New Complete Dog Book: Official Breed Standards and Profiles for Over 200 Breeds* (Mount Joy, PA: Fox Chapel, 2017), 160–63.
[2] "Group Records: Sporting," Westminster Kennel Club, accessed April 2, 2024, https://www.westminsterkennelclub.org/conformation-records/group-records/sporting/.
[3] Reggio, *New Complete Dog Book*, 160–61.
[4] Kathryn Hennessy, ed., *The Dog Encyclopedia: The Definitive Visual Guide* (New York: DK, 2013), 248.

Welsh Terrier

[1] Jan Reisen, "10 Things to Know About Welsh Terriers," American Kennel Club, December 31, 2019, https://www.akc.org/expert-advice/lifestyle/10-facts-about-welsh-terriers/.
[2] "Welsh Terrier," American Kennel Club, https://www.akc.org/dog-breeds/welsh-terrier/.

West Highland White Terrier

[1] "West Highland White Terrier," Dogtime, https://dogtime.com/dog-breeds/west-highland-white-terrier#/slide/1.
[2] "Group Records: Terrier," Westminster Kennel Club, accessed April 2, 2024, https://www.westminsterkennelclub.org/conformation-records/group-records/terrier/.
[3] Kathryn Hennessy, ed., *The Dog Encyclopedia: The Definitive Visual Guide* (New York: DK, 2013), 168.

Notes

Whippet

[1] Rebecca O'Connell, "10 Quick Facts About Whippets," Mental Floss, October 26, 2015, https://www.mentalfloss.com/article/70270/10-quick-facts-about-whippets.

Wire Fox Terrier

[1] Christopher Reggio, ed., *The New Complete Dog Book: Official Breed Standards and Profiles for Over 200 Breeds* (Mount Joy, PA: Fox Chapel, 2017).

[2] "Group Records: Terrier," Westminster Kennel Club, accessed April 2, 2024, https://www.westminsterkennelclub.org/conformation-records/group-records/terrier/.

[3] Reggio, *New Complete Dog Book*, 526.

[4] Reggio, *New Complete Dog Book*, 547.

[5] Kathryn Hennessy, ed., *The Dog Encyclopedia: The Definitive Visual Guide* (New York: DK, 2013), 209.

Yorkshire Terrier

[1] Jan Reisen, "6 Things We Bet You Didn't Know About Yorkshire Terriers," American Kennel Club, November 22, 2020, https://www.akc.org/expert-advice/lifestyle/7-things-about-yorkshire-terriers/.

Dog Groups as Recognized by the American Kennel Club

[1] "The 7 AKC Dog Breed Groups Explained," American Kennel Club, last modified June 14, 2023, https://www.akc.org/expert-advice/lifestyle/7-akc-dog-breed-groups-explained/.

About the Authors

MICHELLE MEDLOCK ADAMS is an inspirational speaker, a best-selling author, and an award-winning journalist, earning top honors from the Associated Press, the Society of Professional Journalists, and the Hoosier State Press Association, to name a few.

An author of over 100 books with more than 3 million books sold, Michelle is also a *New York Times* best-selling ghostwriter and has won more than 90 industry awards for her own journalistic endeavors, including the prestigious 2023 ECPA Gold Medallion Book of the Year for her children's book *Our God Is Bigger Than That!* Her work has also been honored by the Christian Market Book Awards, the AWSA Golden Scrolls, the Selah Book Awards, the Moonbeam Children's Book Awards, *Christianity Today*, and the Illumination Book Awards in multiple categories.

Since graduating with a journalism degree from Indiana University, Michelle has written more than 1,700 articles for newspapers, magazines, and websites; acted as a stringer for the Associated Press; written for a worldwide ministry; hosted *Joy in Our Town* for the Trinity Broadcasting Network; blogged twice weekly for *Guideposts*; founded and served as president of Platinum Literary Services; and served as an adjunct professor at Taylor University. Today, she is the owner and editor of her own children's book imprint—Wren & Bear Books, a division of End Game Press—and a much sought-after speaker at professional writing conferences and women's retreats all over the United States. When not working on her own assignments, Michelle

About the Authors

ghostwrites articles, blog posts, and books for celebrities, politicians, and some of today's most effective and popular ministers.

Michelle is celebrating her recent releases: *Our God Is Bigger Than That!*, *Love Connects Us All*, *The Christmas Devotional*, and *Fly High*.

Michelle is married to her high school sweetheart, Jeff, and they have two daughters, Abby and Allyson, two sons-in-law, four granddaughters, and two grandsons. She and Jeff share their home in Southern Indiana with two diva dachshunds and two spoiled kitties. When not writing or teaching writing, Michelle enjoys bass fishing, cheering on Indiana University sports teams, watching Doris Day movies, and all things leopard print. www.michellemedlockadams.com

WENDY HINOTE LANIER is a former elementary teacher, award-winning author, and CLASS certified speaker who writes and speaks on a variety of topics related to children, writing, parenting, and Christian living. She writes both fiction and nonfiction for children and articles and devotional pieces for adults. Her writing credits include titles for a variety of publishers as well as articles in online and print publications such as *Highlights for Children* and *Clubhouse Magazine*.

Wendy's educational background includes a BS in speech communication disorders, an MS in speech language pathology, and an MEd in elementary education. As a teacher, Wendy spent more than eighteen years in Texas public and private schools specializing in the areas of science, social studies, and language arts. Some of her favorite times as a teacher include the years she spent as a fourth-grade science teacher.

The quintessential Texan, Wendy firmly believes everything is bigger and better in Texas. Her Texas humor shines through in just about everything she does. And, like most Texans, she loves her fur babies. She is currently mom to two much loved rescue dogs who are the inspiration for many of her devotional pieces and Bible study lessons. Both dogs were throwaways whose lives dramatically changed for the better the day they became part of the Lanier household. They spend their days doing pretty much as they please while being waited on hand and foot by Wendy and her husband of more than thirty-five years. https://wendyhinotelanier.com/

Also by
Michelle Medlock Adams

Available at IronStreamMedia.com
or wherever books are sold.